"RUSSICA" BIBLIOGRAPHY SERIES
No. 5

WOJCIECH ZALEWSKI

FUNDAMENTALS OF RUSSIAN REFERENCE WORK IN THE HUMANITIES AND SOCIAL SCIENCES

FOREWORD BY PROF. TERENCE EMMONS

RUSSICA PUBLISHERS, INC.
NEW YORK • 1985

WOJCIECH ZALEWSKI

FUNDAMENTALS OF RUSSIAN REFERENCE WORK IN THE HUMANITIES AND SOCIAL SCIENCES

Russica Bibliography Series, No. 5.

Photograph on back cover by *Brigitte Carnochan.*

Library of Congress Catalog Card Number: 85-42728
ISBN: 0-89830-097-5

RUSSICA PUBLISHERS, INC.
799 Broadway. New York, N. Y. 10003. USA.

DEDICATION - - ACKNOWLEDGEMENT

This work is dedicated to Professor Terence Emmons of Stanford University, my first teacher of Russian bibliography and a supporter of my bibliographic contributions made to THE RUSSIAN REVIEW under his editorship. Several sections from my bibliographic survey published there are adapted for this work. I am dedicating this work, in addition, to Professor Wayne S. Vucinich, Chairman of the Committee for Russian and East European Studies at Stanford, who introduced and promoted courses in Russian bibliography; to Professor William M. Todd III, Chairman of the Department of Slavic Languages and Literatures, who introduced those courses into required offerings of the Department; to other members of the History and Slavic Departments who supported and promoted my bibliographic endeavors; and to my students, who contributed to my bibliographic growth.

I am especially grateful to the Committee for Russian and East European Studies for financial support, to Wendy Bracewell and Vera Shamelis for their editorial assistance, and to Jacek Snopkiewicz for technical help.

TABLE OF CONTENTS

Foreword 1

Introduction 3

PART I GENERAL 4

1. Publishing and its history 4
1.1. Historiography 5
1.2. Soviet publishing 9

2. Bibliography: theory and history 10
2.1. Theory of bibliography 11
2.2. History of bibliography 12
2.2.1. Pre-revolutionary period 12
2.2.2. Soviet period 17

3. Libraries, archives, museums 25
3.1. Libraries 25
3.1.1. Histories of libraries 25
3.1.2. Bibliography on libraries and librarianship 28
3.1.3. Library catalogs 29
3.1.3.1. General 29
3.1.3.2. Manuscript books 31
3.1.3.3. Imprints up to 1800 32
3.1.3.4. Private collections 33
3.1.3.5. Periodical collections 34
3.1.4. Directories of libraries 35
3.2. Archives 35
3.2.1. Literature about archives 35
3.2.2. General guides and textbooks 37
3.2.3. Lists of archival holdings 38
3.3. Guides to Western collections 39
3.4. Museums 40

4. General bibliographies 42
4.1. Textbooks 42
4.2. Guides 43
4.3. Bibliographies of bibliographies 45
4.4. National bibliography 48
4.5. Regional bibliographies (Kraevedcheskaia bibliografiia) 51

4.6. Format bibliographies 54
4.6.1. Books 54
4.6.2. Serials 57
4.6.2.1. Histories of periodicals 57
4.6.2.2. Lists of periodicals 58
4.6.2.2.1. Bibliography of bibliographies 58
4.6.2.2.2. Lists 58
4.6.2.3. Indexes to periodicals 59
4.6.2.3.1. Bibliographies of indexes 59
4.6.2.3.2. Indexes 60
4.6.2.4. Directories of periodicals 60
4.6.3. Dissertations (typescripts) 60
4.6.4. Manuscripts 62
4.7. Publisher's bibliographies 62
4.8. Western language materials 64
4.8.1. Catalogs 64
4.8.2. Current bibliographies 64
4.8.3. Retrospective bibliographies 65
4.8.4. Serials 65
4.9. Émigré publications 65
4.9.1. Monographs 65
4.9.2. Serials 66
4.9.2.1. Lists 66
4.9.2.2. Indexes 67

5. Non-bibliographic reference sources (Spravochniki) 68
5.1. Bibliography 68
5.2. Encyclopedias 68
5.2.1. General 68
5.2.2. Subject encyclopedias 70
5.2.2.3. English language subject encyclopedias: a selection 73
5.3. Biographical sources 73
5.3.1. Bibliography 73
5.3.2. General sources 73
5.3.3. Government and political Leaders 74
5.3.4. Writers 75
5.3.5. Scholars and scientists 76
5.3.6. Artists 77
5.3.7. Film and Stage personalities 77
5.3.8. Musicians 78
5.4. Linguistic dictionaries 78
5.5. Dictionary of Pseudonyms 78
5.6. Statistics 78
5.6.1. Bibliographies 78
5.6.1.1. Russian Pre-1917 78

5.6.1.2. Soviet 79
5.6.2. Selected Russian statistical publications 79
5.6.3. Selected Soviet statistical publications 80
5.6.4. Histories of statistics 81
5.6.5. Western statistics on the Soviet Union 81
5.6.5.1. Bibliographies 81
5.6.5.2. Selected statistical sources 81
5.7. Geographic sources 82
5.7.1. Bibliographies 82
5.7.2. Non-bibliographic sources 83
5.8. Directories 83
5.8.1. Bibliography 83
5.8.2. Business 83
5.8.3. Academic Institutions 84
5.8.4. City directories 84
5.9. Current events 85
5.10. Political quides, events, data 85

PART II
SUBJECT (OTRASLEVYE) BIBLIOGRAPHIES 86

1. Soviet bibliographic institutions 88
1.1. Institut Nauchnoi Informatsii po Obshchestvennym Naukam at the USSR Academy of Sciences. (UNION). Formerly Fundamental'naia Biblioteka po Obshchestvennym Naukam. (FBON). 88
1.2. Informatsionnyi Tsentr po Problemam Kul'tury i Iskusstva 95

2.History 97
2.1. Publishing 97
2.2. Libraries, archives, museums 97
2.3. Textbooks, guides, bibliographies of bibliographies 98
2.4. General bibliographies 99
2.4.1. Pre-1917 imprints 100
2.4.1.1. Vladimir Izmailovich Mezhov (1830-1894) 100
2.4.1.2. Bibliography 101
2.4.2. Soviet period 102
2.5. Indexes to periodicals 104
2.6. Current bibliographies 105
2.7. Special bibliographies 105

2.7.1. Historiography 106
2.7.2. Source study
(arkheografiia, istochnikovedenie) 106
2.7.3. History of Sciences and Technology 108
2.8. Western languages 109
2.9. Non-bibliographic reference sources 110
2.9.1. Companion to history 111
2.9.2. Chronology 111
2.9.3. Dictionaries 111
2.9.4. Atlases 111
2.9.5. Governmental institutions 111

3. Literature 113
3.1. Publishing 113
3.2. Libraries, Archives, Museums 117
3.3. Textbooks, guides, bibliographies
of bibliographies 119
3.4. General bibliographies 121
3.5. Indexes to periodicals, serials,
literary almanacs, collections
of papers 125
3.6. Current bibliographies 127
3.7. Russian literature and criticism
in Western languages 129
3.8. Émigré literature 132
3.9. Special Bibliographies 132
3.9.1. Textology 133
3.9.2. Folklore 133
3.9.3. Comparative literature 133
3.10. Non-bibliographic reference sources 134

4. Russian linguistics and language studies 135
4.1. Institutions 135
4.2. History of language studies 136
4.3. Bibliographies of bibliographies 136
4.4. General linguistics and language studies 137
4.5. Slavic (including Russian) language
studies 138
4.6. Russian language 139
4.7. Indexes 140
4.8. Bibliography of dictionaries 140

5. Social sciences 142
5.1. Social sciences in general 142
5.2. Archeology 142
5.3. Ethnography 143
5.4. Economy 143
5.5. Education 144

5.6. Law 145
5.6.1. Bibliography of bibliographies and reference works 145
5.6.2. Pre-revolutionary law 145
5.6.3. Soviet law, with Nelli Houke 146
Research and publication in juridical sciences by Nelli Houke 146
Bibliographies 148
Academic textbooks 148
5.7. Sociology 149

6. The Humanities (other than history, literature, language) 150
6.1. Art 150
6.2. Theater, drama 151
6.3. Music 152
6.4. Film 154
6.5. Philosophy 155
6.6. Religion 155

INDEX 156

APPENDIX. Serials: Terminology and current monographic numbered series published in the West, by Alla Avisov 163

FOREWORD

It is a pleasure to present this, the most substantial contribution to Russian bibliography to date by Wojciech Zalewski, Curator for Russian and East European Collections at Stanford University Libraries.

For almost a decade now, Mr. Zalewski has been introducing beginning graduate students at Stanford to Russian reference work in an annual course, and publishing his annual survey of reference materials in Russian/Soviet area studies in the pages of the RUSSIAN REVIEW. The experience accumulated in those two enterprizes is clearly reflected in the following pages. As the author points out in his Introduction, this work both updates and enhances the value of existing reference works. It is worth noting, however, that bibliographies of bibliographies, the starting point for any systematic bibliographic search, have been few and far between in the Russian field: as a matter of fact, the first substantial Soviet general bibliography of bibliographies was published only in 1983: Boris L. Kandel', OTECHESTVENNYE UKAZATELI BIBLIOGRAFICHESKIKH POSOBII. Until its appearence there were only two such general bibliographies available, both, interestingly enough, prepared for an Anglo-American readership and the first of them also prepared at Stanford: Karol Maichel, GUIDE TO RUSSIAN REFERENCE WORKS (1962-); and John S.G. Simmons, RUSSIAN BIBLIOGRAPHY, LIBRARIES AND ARCHIVES (1973).

The present work does not replace these pioneering efforts, for we shall go on consulting Maichel's invaluable annotations and Simmons's superbly selected and organized list. It does of course update them, and, especially importanty, it enhances their value by providing explicit guidance to the "structure of the reference network" (Introduction) and suggestions on how to design bibliographic searches. It is, to my knowledge, the first published work to combine the features of substantial general bibliography-reference work and guide to research for Russian studies as a whole, and thus fills a longstanding need of beginning scholars (but not only beginning scholars) who, most of them, do not enjoy access to an ongoing course of instruction on Russian bibliography. All toilers in the field of Russian studies are in the author's debt.

Terence Emmons
Department of History
Stanford University

INTRODUCTION

In spite of the growing number of commercial data bases, machine readable data tapes, and other online information sources, the traditional printed bibliography is still essential for research in many fields, and it will continue to be produced by scholars, bibliographers, and institutions. This is particularly true for Soviet studies, for which the advent of automated information sources has been slow.

This reference book introduces the network of bibliographic and reference sources for Russian studies. As a starting point, one should gain an understanding of the structure and interrelations of these works by reading their introductions and reviews of them. In addition, since bibliography is a part of a larger book culture (publishing, the book trade, libraries and archives, in Russian knigovedenie and knizhnoe delo), knowledge of the different components of this book culture will also help to understand the bibliographic work done in a given historic period and to evaluate bibliographic production, layer upon layer, through time. Such an understanding is the basis for efficient and effective bibliographic research.

The primary purpose of this book is to provide overall reference guidance by introducing users to the structure of the reference network. It builds on already existing reference books. Rather than repeating titles listed in them it refers to them, relates them to one another, and updates them. In addition, it lists the crucial stepping stones in the bibliographic process and offers methodological suggestions for a bibliographic search. This work grew out of classroom practice, and it is hoped that it will serve an educational role.

PART I

GENERAL

1. Publishing and its history

Publishing and bibliography go hand in hand. Consequently a knowledge of the structure and history of the publishing industry of a country is a prerequisite to understanding its bibliographic network. For example, the fact that manuscript books were produced in Russia through the eighteenth century and that printing at that time lay exclusively in Church and state hands splits the bibliographies into two distinct categories: those of manuscript books and those of printed works. Similarly, scholarly institutions conducting and publishing their research produce bibliographies of their imprints; and nationalized publishing in the Soviet Union lays the foundation for thoroughness in the national bibliography and influences the quality of subject bibliographies based on it. On the other hand bibliographies aid the study of the history of publishing because they alow us to assess the publishing output for a particular time or field of knowledge. Existing bibliographies do not cover the heritage of manuscript and printed books comprehensively. This has resulted in lacunae in the research on the Russian book culture. Nevertheless, bibliography should be studied in the broader context of the book culture since the understanding of the whole cultural environment facilitates more efficient use of bibliographies.

1.1. Historiography

The book as a subject of scholarly investigation began to attract Russian scholars in the second half of the nineteenth century. Although the bibliography of works devoted to this subject is quite impressive (see Mez'er below), comprehensive studies have not been undertaken. A brief overview of research on book culture is given by V. Ia. Adariukov and A. A. Sidorov, RUSSKAIA KNIGA OT NACHALA PIS'MENNOSTI DO 1800 GODA (Moscow, Gosudarstvennoe izdatel'stvo, 1924:5-6), the first of three volumes planned under the title KNIGA V ROSSII. The project was intended to provide a scholarly compendium on the history of the book in Russia. However, these prominent scholars, who represent pre-revolutionary academic traditions, could not advance their work beyond volume one. The second volume: RUSSKAIA KNIGA DEVIATNADTSATOGO VEKA (published in 1925) was no longer a survey but a collection of articles. The bibliography announced in volumes one and three never appeared. Research done in the Soviet Union on the history of books and publishing is extensive. Guidelines for systematic work on the book culture were established at the First All-Union Conference on "The Book in Russia to the Mid-Nineteenth Century" (Leningrad, October 1976). The conference papers were published in KNIGA V ROSSII DO SEREDINY XIX VEKA (Leningrad, Akademiia Nauk SSSR, 1978). The second conference (Leningrad, April 23-25, 1981) reinforced earlier decisions. The proceedings of the second conference can be found in B.B. Piotrovskii, S.P. Luppov, eds. RUSSKIE BIBLIOTEKI I IKH CHITATEL'. IZ ISTORII RUSSKOI KUL'TURY EPOKHI FEODALIZMA (Leningrad, [Biblioteka AN SSSR](BAN), 1983.) Included is a historiography of studies on the history of the book, listing works since 1976.

The first conference commissioned the Library of the Academy of Sciences in Leningrad to work on the Russian manuscript book culture. Because some of the manuscript materials were already under bibliographic control in published catalogs of library collections, several publications of historical scope have been possible since then: B. V. Sapunov, KNIGA V ROSSII V XI-XIII VV. (Leningrad, Nauka, 1978); N. N. Rozov, KNIGA DREVNEI RUSI XI-XIV VV. (Moscow, Kniga, 1977); and

Rozov's KNIGA V ROSSII V XV VEKE (Leningrad, Nauka, 1981). These three works discuss books, their dissemination, ownership, readership, and libraries. Rozov's books contain valuable supplements, one of which has a list of fifteenth century books continuing E. F. Karskii, "Perechen' datirovannykh russkikh knig XI-XIV vv." in SLAVIANSKAIA KIRILLOVSKAIA PALEOGRAFIIA (Moscow, Nauka, 1979:44-52).

The leading researcher of the early period of printing in Russia is E. L. Nemirovskii, who is associated with the Lenin Public Library in Moscow. His works include the monograph VOZNIKNOVENIE KNIGOPECHATANIIA V MOSKVE. IVAN FEDOROV (Moscow, [Gos. Biblioteka SSSR im. V.I. Lenina] (MPB), 1964) and the extensive bibliography NACHALO KNIGOPECHATANIIA V MOSKVE I NA UKRAINE. ZHIZN' I DEIATEL'NOST' PERVOPECHATNIKA IVANA FEDOROVA: UKAZATEL' LITERATURY, 1574-1974 (Moscow, [MBP], 1975). Other studies, catalogs, and bibliographies that register early imprints have also contributed significantly to our knowledge of the sixteenth century Russian book.

The Academy of Sciences' work on the history of the book in the seventeenth and eighteenth centuries is represented by: S.P. Luppov, KNIGA V ROSSII V XVII VEKE (Leningrad, Nauka, 1973), KNIGA V ROSSII V PERVOI CHETVERTI XVIII VEKA (Leningrad, Nauka, 1973), KNIGA V ROSSII V POSLEPETROVSKOE VREMIA, 1725-1740 (Leningrad, Nauka, 1976), KNIGA V ROSSII DO SEREDINY XIX VEKA (Leningrad, Nauka, 1978), to be continued. The period most lacking in coverage is the nineteenth and early twentieth centuries, primary research responsibility for which rests with the Saltykov-Shchedrin Public Library in Leningrad (SS). The library is beginning its work with a major monograph covering the second half of the nineteenth century to the revolution, and some information on this topic can already be found in KNIZHNOE DELO I BIBLIOGRAFIIA V ROSSII VTOROI POLOVINY XIX-NACHALA XX VEKA (Leningrad, [BAN], 1980). The extensive collections of nineteenth-century Russian imprints available in the West make this an ideal topic for Western contributions.

The Lenin Public Library in Moscow (MPB) has been commissioned to work on the Soviet period. The library has published catalogs on selected segments of its collections and has also sponsored several conferences with the proceedings published in KNIGA I KUL'TURA (Moscow, [BAN], 1979) and SOVETSKAIA ISTORIOGRAFIIA KNIGI (Moscow, [BAN], 1979). It is planning to publish a multivolume history of Soviet books for the period 1917-1977. The first volume, M.P. Kim, ed., ISTORIIA KNIGI V SSSR. TOM 1. 1917-1921 (Moscow, Kniga, 1983), has just appeared. The introduction includes the historiography of Russian printing and a survey of sources.

Textbooks are:

400 LET RUSSKOGO KNIGOPECHATANIIA. 1564-1964. Moscow, Nauka, 1964. 2 vols.

Barenbaum, I.E., Davydova, T.E. ISTORIIA KNIGI. Moscow, Kniga, 1971.
2nd ed. Moscow, Kniga, 1984.

Malykhin, N.G. OCHERKI PO ISTORII IZDATEL'SKOGO DELA V SSSR. Moscow, Kniga, 1965.

Nazarov, A.I. OCHERKI ISTORII SOVETSKOGO KNIGOIZDATEL'STVA. Moscow, Iskusstvo, 1952.

Govorov, A.A. ISTORIIA KNIZHNOI TORGOVLI V SSSR. Moscow, Kniga, 1982. (Earlier eds. 1965 and 1976.)

Western contributions on Russian and Soviet publishing are:

Simmons, J.S.G. "Printing" in A. Auty, D. Obolensky, eds. AN INTRODUCTION TO RUSSIAN LANGUAGE AND LITERATURE. Cambridge, Eng., Cambridge University Press, [n.d.], pp. 47-55 (COMPANION TO RUSSIAN STUDIES, 2).

Gorokhoff, B.I. PUBLISHING IN THE USSR. Bloomington, Ind., 1959 (SLAVIC AND EAST EUROPEAN SERIES, XIX).

Walker, G.P.M. SOVIET BOOK PUBLISHING POLICY. Cambridge, Eng., Cambridge University Press, 1978.

Bibliographies of the history of books are:

Mez'er, A.V. SLOVARNYI UKAZATEL' PO KNIGOVEDENIIU. Leningrad, Kolos, 1924: 443-471 and vol. 2, Moscow, Gos. Sotsial'no-ekonomicheskoe izdatel'stvo, 1933: 249-274.

400 LET RUSSKOGO KNIGOPECHATANIIA. 1564-1964. Vol. 1, pp.633-650, vol. 2, pp. 552-564.

Nemirovskii, E.L. NACHALO KNIGOPECHATANIIA V MOSKVE I NA UKRAINE. ZHIZN' I DEIATEL'NOST' PERVOPECHATNIKA IVANA FEDOROVA. UKAZATEL' LITERATURY. 1574-1974. Moscow, [MPB], 1975.

Belov, S.V. KNIGA V ROSSII (1850-1971). MATERIALY K UKAZATELIU SOVETSKOI LITERATURY. 1917-1977. Moscow, [MPB],1979.

Podomazova, T.A., Egorova, L.E. SOVETSKAIA KNIGA. UKAZATEL' LITERATURY O KNIGE I KNIZHNOM DELE. Chast' 1. KNIGA I KNIZHNOE DELO V PERVYE GODY SOVETSKOI VLASTI. Moscow, [MPB], 1976. 2 vols. Chast' 2. KNIGA I KNIZHNOE DELO V SSSR 1922-1931 GG. UKAZATEL' LITERATURY. Moscow, [MPB], 1979. Chast' 3. Vyp. 1. KNIGA I KNIZHNOE DELO V SSSR 1932-1945 GG. UKAZATEL' LITERATURY. Moscow, [MPB], 1982.
(Compilers changed for various volumes).

Nemirovskii, E.L. PROBLEMY KNIGOVEDENIIA. ISTORIIA KNIZHNOGO DELA. OBZOR LITERATURY 1964-1969 GG. Moscow, Kniga, 1970.

SOVETSKAIA ISTORIOGRAFIIA KNIGI. SBORNIK NAUCHNYKH TRUDOV. Moscow, [MPB], 1979.

"Sovetskaia literatura (1966-1975) po istorii russkoi knigi do serediny XIX v.," in KNIGA V ROSSII DO SEREDINY XIX VEKA. A.A. Sidorov, S.P. Luppov, eds. Leningrad, Nauka, 1978. Continued by "Sovetskaia literatura (1976-1981) po istorii russkoi knigi do serediny XIX v.," in RUSSKIE BIBLIOTEKI I IKH CHITATEL'(IZ ISTORII RUSSKOI KUL'TURY EPOKHI FEODALIZMA). B.B. Piotrovskii, S.P. Luppov, eds. Leningrad, Nauka, 1983: 235-239.

Podomazova, T.A., et al. ARKHIVNYE MATERIALY PO ISTORII KNIGI I KNIZHNOGO DELA SSSR, 1917-1977 GG. UKAZATEL'. Moscow, [MPB], 1975.

Podomazova, T.A., et al. ARKHIVNYE MATERIALY PO ISTORII KNIGI I KNIZHNOGO DELA SSSR, 1917-1977 GG. UKAZATEL'. Chast' 1. KRAEVYE I OBLASTNYE ARKHIVY. Moscow, [MPB], 1980.

KNIGA. ISSLEDOVANIIA I MATERIALY, 1959- Includes yearly bibliographies.

KNIGOVEDENIE. ENTSIKLOPEDICHESKII SLOVAR'. Moscow, Sovetskaia entsiklopediia, 1982.

1.2. Soviet publishing

No book systematically discusses the whole spectrum of issues dealing with publishing in the Soviet Union. Perhaps G.P.M. Walker, op. cit.,is the most useful source for a general understanding of the structure of Soviet publishing. Soviet sources such as I.E. Barenbaum, op. cit., articles on "Izdatel'skoe delo" and on various publishing houses in the encyclopedia KNIGOVEDENIE, and 400 LET RUSSKOGO KNIGOPECHATANIIA, vol. 2, also provide general data. A.E. Mil'chin, ed., KRATKII SPRAVOCHNIK KNIGOLIUBA. 3rd ed. (Moscow, Kniga, 1976), lists publishing houses, including their addresses. The bibliographies on book history listed above provide access to additional sources.

Publishing in the Soviet Union has undergone several reorganizations. I.E. Barenbaum, op. cit., outlines them concisely. Discussion of some of the most recent changes can be found in V.A. Markus, "Novye normativnye materialy v izdatel'skom dele (1977-1982 gg.)," KNIGA. ISSLEDOVANIIA I MATERIALY. SBORNIK 47, 1983:18-28, with reference to the earlier survey on this subject.

The present publishing organization includes:

a. The Party's own publishing house. It issues, among other things, the newspaper PRAVDA, journals, and monographs.

b. Publishing houses under the State Committee for Publishing, Printing, and the Book Trade (Gosudarstvennyi Komitet Soveta Ministrov SSSR po delam izdatel'stv, poligrafii i knizhnoi torgovli

[Goskomizdat]). These houses, primarily discipline-oriented, constitute the core of Soviet publishing.
c. Publishing houses reporting to Goskomizdat and another organization, for example, the Ministry of Education. Among these is the publishing house Nauka.
d. Publishing houses of societies, ministries, and departments (vedomstva).
e. Institutions with rights to publish, e.g., pedagogical institutes. Although they are not formal publishing houses, they issue about 40 percent of the titles published in the USSR annually and reported in publishing statistics. The very small number of copies in which they are issued and the fact that they are not distributed commercially result in problems of availability, and the frequent changes of series titles (uchenye zapiski, trudy, sborniki, etc.) complicates bibliographic control.

2. Bibliography: theory and history

The definition of bibliography as an independent discipline is still disputed. Therefore, instead of engaging in an analysis of the theoretical principles of bibliography, this work will take a practical approach and discuss bibliography as a dynamic process of registering and retrieving information. The process begins with identification of information. This information is then recorded according to bibliographic standards and methodologies. It is organized in subject, geographical, chronological, or merely alphabetical order, according to the purpose of the compiler, by the methods traditionally used for certain types of bibliographies or by a particular discipline. Once an initial registration is made, it may serve as a resource in other bibliographic projects. Thus a bibliographic network composed of interwoven and interrelated parts has been created. The ability to use this network is enhanced by the researcher's understanding of the principles upon which the network was built.

2.1. Theory of bibliography

The theory of bibliography will not be discussed below. Those interested in it will find some aspects indicated in the chapter on the history of bibliography. Soviet bibliographers have a strong interest in theoretical aspects of bibliography. This is documented in such works as A.I. Barsuk, O.P. Korshunov, SOVETSKOE BIBLIOGRAFOVEDENIE: SOSTOIANIE, PROBLEMY, PERSPEKTIVY (Moscow, Kniga, 1977) and O.P. Korshunov, PROBLEMY OBSHCHEI TEORII BIBLIOGRAFII (Moscow, Kniga, 1975). This research found its practical application in the academic textbook edited by O.P. Korshunov, BIBLIOGRAFIIA. OBSHCHII KURS (Moscow, Kniga, 1981), which supersedes earlier publications of similar scope: M.A. Briskman, A.D. Eikhengol'ts, eds., BIBLIOGRAFIIA. OBSHCHII KURS (Moscow, Kniga, 1969) and G.N. Diomidova, A.I. Barsuk, BIBLIOGRAFIIA. OBSHCHII KURS (Moscow, Kniga, 1978). Korshunov emphasizes the social functions of bibliography, international bibliographic cooperation, bibliographic forms, and the contemporary organization of bibliographic work in the Soviet Union. He devotes less attention than his predecessor Briskman to the history of bibliography.

The leading journal discussing the theory and history of bibliography is SOVETSKAIA BIBLIOGRAFIIA (SB), (1933- ,6 issues per year). The journal is also a main source for reviews of bibliographies.

The index to SOVETSKAIA BIBLIOGRAFIIA is

Alferova, L.N., Kasabova, B.N. SOVETSKAIA BIBLIOGRAFIIA. SISTEMATICHESKII UKAZATEL' SODERZHANIIA (1933-1970). Moscow, Kniga, 1972.

Bibliographies dealing with the theory of bibliography are:

Masanov, Iu. I. TEORIIA I PRAKTIKA BIBLIOGRAFII. UKAZATEL' LITERATURY, 1917-1958. Moscow, [VKP], 1960.

BIBLIOTEKOVEDENIE I BIBLIOGRAFIIA. UKAZATEL' LITERATURY. Moscow, 1959-

"Bibliografovedenie" in SOVETSTKAIA BIBLIOGRAFIIA, 1982- annually.

2.2. History of bibliography

Sources:

Ianovskii, A.E., "Bibliografiia", ENTSIKLOPEDICHESKII SLOVAR' BROKHAUS-EFRON. St. Petersburg, 1891, vol. 3, pp. 720-769.

Zdobnov, N.V. ISTORIIA RUSSKOI BIBLIOGRAFII DO NACHALA XX V. 3rd ed.by B.S. Bodnarskii. Moscow, Gos. izd. kul'turno-prosvetitel'noi literatury, 1955.

Mashkova, M.V. ISTORIIA RUSSKOI BIBLIOGRAFII NACHALA XX V. (DO OKTIABRIA 1917 G). Moscow, Kniga, 1969.

See also the textbooks by M.A. Briskman, op. cit. and O.P. Korshunov, op. cit.

Bibliographies about the activities of bibliographers can be found in:

Iu. I. Masanov, op. cit. and

Kandel', B.L. OTECHESTVENNYE UKAZATELI BIBLIOGRAFICHESKIKH POSOBII. Leningrad, [SS], 1983:223-247.

2.2.1. Pre-revolutionary period

Russian bibliography developed along a few very distinct lines: library catalogs, later book dealers' catalogs, retrospective bibliographies, and bibliographies of current publications.

Up to the reign of Peter the Great, Russian intellectual life was centered mainly around the monasteries of the Orthodox Church. Therefore, the first efforts in bibliography were the library catalogs. Among the most important of these are the catalogs of such monasteries as Cyril-Belozersk and Volokolamsk. The expansion of printing activities and the intellectual and religious revival started under the patriarch Nikon created a need for better documentation. This resulted in the first union catalog of thirty-nine monasteries published in 1653. This catalog also included books from the very impressive private library of the Patriarch. In 1742-1744 the Library of the Academy of Sciences published its catalog, an important bibliographic tool for its time. Toward the end of the eighteenth and the beginning of the nineteenth centuries many wealthy Russians such as A. Golovkin, A. Razumovskii, and P. Demidov published catalogs of their private collections. These catalogs were especially valuable from a bibliophilic point of view and are important sources for the study of the history of Russian culture. Undoubtedly the most outstanding bibliographic achievements of nineteenth century Russia are the catalog of Russica in the St. Petersburg Public Library (1873) and the catalog of the library of St. Petersburg University (1897-1902). The latter publication is considered one of the best retrospective bibliographic sources for nineteenth century Russian publications and both are useful research tools even today.

The organized book business started in Russia in 1708 with the opening in Moscow of V. Kiprianov's bookstore. Two years later, Kiprianov set up a printing office and bookstore in St. Petersburg. Commercial book lists, however, did not appear until 1728 when the Academy of Sciences established its own bookstore. The Academy's book lists were of scholarly, as well as commercial, value. This characteristic is typical for the majority of Russian nineteenth century bibliographies.

The intense intellectual activity which occurred especially between 1767 and 1789 created a favorable climate for the expansion of the book business. In the 1780's there were twenty bookstores in Moscow and fifteen in St. Peterburg. Many scholars were directly involved in book dissemination, the most prominent being Nikolai I. Novikov, a scholar, journalist, and manager of the bookstore at Moscow University. He and others such as Fedor Kochetov opened public reading rooms in their bookstores and published their catalogs in thousands of copies. The outstanding bibliographic work of V.G. Anastasevich,a catalog of the holdings of V.A. Plavil'shchikov's combined printing office, bookstore, library, and "literary club" had similar beginnings. It was first issued from 1817 to 1820 and was updated when the bookstore came under the ownership of A.F. Smirdin in 1828. This nearly comprehensive compilation of Russian publications is still a valuable bibliographic source. Later supplements issued when the store was owned by P.I. Krasheninnikov extended the bibliographic registration up to 1856. Another important source of this type was prepared for the Ol'khin bookstore from 1831 to 1846.

In the second half of the nineteenth century, book dealers hired the best bibliographers available to compile their catalogs. The most outstanding examples of these professionally prepared catalogs were those issued by the two largest book outlets in Russia: Glazunov and Bazunov. The Glazunov catalog, compiled by P.A. Efremov, covered imprints published between 1856 and 1866 with supplements up to 1887. The catalog of the Bazunov book firm and its six supplements were prepared by V.I. Mezhov and covered publications printed up to 1874. In addition to books, it also contained articles and reviews for the period 1825 to 1869 and was equipped with a subject index. Both of these features were innovative. The catalogs of the Isakov and Vol'f bookstores are also of value. Increased book production and the specialization of bookstores in the 1890's made further compilation of this type of comprehensive listing infeasible. It should be noted that, in their time, the commercially prepared catalogs were the best bibliographies available.

In addition to the bookstore catalogs, the only nearly comprehensive bibliography of retrospective materials is the bibliography by V.S. Sopikov (1813-1821), covering the sixteenth to the eighteenth centuries. This work is of great value to scholars of this period.

Many specialized subject bibliographies began to appear in the second half of the nineteenth century. Among these are bibliographies of history by Mezhov and the Lambin brothers, of literature by Mezhov and A.V. Mez'er, and works on periodicals by A.N. Neustroev (covering 1703-1802) and V.A. Popov (for the period 1830-1884). S A. Ven-gerov's ambitious project to compile a comprehensive bibliography of Russian nineteenth century imprints (RUSSKIE KNIGI. S BIOGRAFICHESKIMI DANNYMI OB AVTORAKH I PEREVODCHIKAKH (1708-1897).

St.Petersburg, G.V. Iudin, 1897-1898. 3 vols.) reached only the third letter of the Russian alphabet (Vavilov).

The Russian intelligentsia's keen interest in books was expressed in critical reviews printed in all of the leading journals. It is a fact that the quality of the review section often determined the prestige and commercial success of a journal and was used as a competitive means for attracting readers. The listing of books in periodicals started with the first Russian newspaper, VEDOMOSTI. In 1710, VEDOMOSTI published a supplement which listed books printed since 1708 in the secular alphabet under Peter the Great. (Peter the Great introduced the secular alphabet in 1708. It was a modernized form of the ecclesiastical type of the Cyrillic alphabet. The new alphabet became mandatory for books on secular subjects.) The purpose of this "bibliography" was to hail the Tsar for his cultural patronage. Critical bibliographies of current materials began only with the publication of RUSSISCHE BIBLIOTHEK... in 1772. The first journal devoted strictly to analytical and systematic bibliography was ULEI, founded and edited by V.G. Anastasevich in 1811-1812. Anastasevich's journal compiled a register of current imprints based on the mandatory submission copy of all Russian publications to the St. Petersburg Public Library. The mandatory submission law went into effect in 1810. Beginning with SYN OTECHESTVA, edited by N.I. Grech', 1814-1839, all the leading journals printed critical bibliographies. Among the numerous periodicals of the nineteenth-century, MOSKOVSKII TELEGRAF, edited by N.A. Polevoi, 1825-1834, SOVREMENNIK, edited consecutively by A.S. Pushkin, V.G. Belinskii, N.A. Nekrasov, N.G. Chernyshevskii, and N.A. Dobroliubov, 1836-1864, OTECHESTVENNYE ZAPISKI under A.A. Kraevskii, 1839-1864, and BIBLIOTEKA DLIA CHTENIIA edited, by O.I. Senkovskii, 1834-1864, contained the best reviews, critical notes, and annotations. The reviews published in these journals were often vehicles for unorthodox ideas that clashed with the views of the tsarist censorship. Toward the end of the nineteenth century numerous journals were devoted either to general or specialized bibliographies, e.g., science, children's literature, etc. These journals developed bibliography to a high art, ranging from the scholarly and critical through popular to commercial.

In 1826 a law was passed requiring the preliminary censorship of each article submitted for publication to newspapers and journals. In practice, this law was also applied to books. The censor's reports facilitated the production of book lists which appeared as "Ukazatel' vnov' vykhodiashchikh knig..." (List of newly published books) in ZHURNAL MINISTERSTVA NARODNOGO PROSVESHCHENIIA, starting in 1837. This compilation was nearly comprehensive. After the death of Nicholas I in 1855, censorship became less rigid and the "Ukazatel'" was abolished. The task of listing current publications was taken up by KNIZHNYI VESTNIK, which functioned from 1860-1868 as a private enterprise. The mandatory copy submitted to the St. Petersburg Public Library became once again the basis for the bibliography. Although the government exempted all books from preliminary censorship in 1865, punitive censorship was strengthened. This move required a good overview of publishing activities. Official registration restarted in 1869 in the newspaper PRAVITEL'STVENNYI VESTNIK and continued until 1903 (except for 1877-1878). The years from 1884 to 1902 were also published separately as SPISOK IZDANII, VYSHEDSHIKH V ROSSII (LIST OF PUBLICATIONS ISSUED IN RUSSIA) by the Central Office for Publications (Glavnoe upravlenie po delam pechati). The bibliographic registration continued even after 1903, i.e., after PRAVITEL'STVENNYI VESTNIK was closed until June 30, 1907 when KNIZHNAIA LETOPIS' (BOOK CHRONICLE) was established. SPISOK (the weekly lists), however, were neither indexed nor cumulated, thus they are difficult to consult now. Since they were intended for use by officials, they were printed only in about 100 copies and therefore could not fill the bibliographic needs of the country. This encouraged the prolific privately sponsored bibliographic literature outlined above.

Beginning in 1907, KNIZHNAIA LETOPIS' (KL) initiated a new era in Russian bibliography. Under the editorship of A.D. Toropov, it was the only current bibliographic listing until 1917. Its bibliographic standards were higher than those of SPISOK. KL, the national bibliography, registered books, selected articles, pamphlets, maps, music scores, serials, and included some titles published abroad. It had both subject and systematic indexes. Its contents were based on the required copy of published materials sent to the Central Office for Publications. Since this office was not interested in government and church publications and was unable to obtain all publications issued outside the main publishing centers of the country, it was not comprehensive.

In conclusion, it may be observed that the intensification of intellectual life in Russia was always accompanied by equally intense bibliographic activities, for example, during the turn of the eighteenth and nineteenth centuries, or the second half of the nineteenth century. The interim periods witnessed commercial and critical bibliographies published in journals.

2.2.2. Soviet period

The changing book scene from pre-revolutionary Russia into a new society still remains poorly researched. The fate of book people who made the transition or disappeared in those tumultuous times is often unknown. Soviet scholarship, although seemingly prolific, has done still very little to answer these questions. The Soviets have published official documents dealing with what they call "knizhnoe delo" some biographies have appeared in the series DEIATELI KNIGI, and textbooks in bibliography have been prepared. Western scholars have also paid limited attention to the history of Soviet bibliography. Only some of the factors which shaped the development of bibliography in the Soviet Union were noted by J.S.G. Simmons in his "Editor's preface" to K. Maichel, GUIDE TO RUSSIAN REFERENCE BOOKS (Stanford, Hoover Institution, 1962; vol.1 and vol.2 contain the same preface).

The historic processes which affected Russian society after the Revolution influenced bibliographic work as well. The forces active at that time are complex and difficult to summarize. For our purpose perhaps it will be useful to take into consideration two main directions: the centralization of the bibliographic work around the main bibliographic institutions (a practical aspect) and the notion of "partiinost'" in bibliography (a theoretical developmental force). Both of them, although enacted centrally, had to find their followers, promotors, and prominence and devoted their lives to scholarly bibliography during the pre-revolutionary era the new environment was difficult to accept. Representatives of that generation were: Semen A. Vengerov (1855-1920), Nikolai M. Lisovskii (1854-1920), Andrei D. Toropov (1851-1927), Augusta V. Mez'er (1869-1935) and others. There were those who worked within the system, but whose independent bibliographic activities lasted only through the early 1930's, for example, Bogdan S. Bodnarskii (1874-1968), and Ignatii V. Vladislavlev (1880-1962). As the Revolution took its toll among bibliographers, new people came to implement Party policies. Important among these were Lev N. Tropovskii (1885-1944), who was responsible for bibliography and libraries at the Narodnyi Komitet Prosveshcheniia from 1923, and Aleksandr D. Eikhengol'ts (1897-1970), Tropovskii's successor at the Moscow Library Institute (now Moscow's Institute of Culture) in 1937, and author of the first textbook in bibliography.

The centralization of bibliographic work began with Lenin's decree of June 30, 1920 "O peredache bibliograficheskogo dela v RSFSR Narodnomu Komissariatu Prosveshcheniia." It subordinated bibliographic activities to the authority of the National Committee for Education, which was responsible primarily for the national registration of published works. As a consequence the Book Chamber was established on August 3, 1920 under the guidance of Bodnarskii. A year later Bodnarskii moved to the Russian Bibliographic Institute, which he founded, and the directorship of the Book Chamber was offered to N.F. Ianitskii. The First All-Russian Bibliographic Congress in 1924 delineated the bibliographic goals, not only of the Book Chamber, but also of other major bibliographic centers and libraries. Thus the national bibliographic network was developed in the 1920's and 1930's, with Vsesoiuznaia Knizhnaia Palata (VKP) (the All Union Book Chamber), as it has been called since 1936, at its head. VKP serves as the compiler and publisher of the national bibliographic series (see 4.4. below), sets bibliographic standards for book chambers of the republics and other bibliographic institutions, and is a center for national cataloging. It cooperates in the preparation of major bibliographies, conducts research in bibliographic theory and methodology, and it prepares the journal SOVETSKAIA BIBLIOGRAFIIA (SB) and the annual publishing statistics in PECHAT' SSSR. It also serves as an archive for all Soviet imprints, and is a major bibliographic center for the party, government, and major research institutions. In addition to the book chambers, all major libraries in the Soviet Union conduct bibliographic work. Central libraries are responsible for bibliographic work in their specializations, e.g. the Saltykov-Shchedrin Public Library in Leningrad is responsible for, among other things, works on the bibliography of bibliographies, Soviet literature, and Russian nineteenth-century comprehensive bibliography (in preparation); the Lenin Public Library in Moscow, for recommendatory bibliographies; the Foreign Literature Library and the Institute of Scientific Information for Social Studies, Moscow, for bibliographies in their respective fields; and public libraries in various regions for materials published in and pertaining to their regions. Major bibliographic works are all prepared as cooperative library ventures.

The concept of partiinost' is the theoretical aspect affecting the profile and content of Soviet bibliography. O.P. Korshunov (BIBLIOGRAFIIA, p.47), today's leading theoretician of Soviet bibliography and head of the Moscow's Institute of Culture, expresses this concept as follows: "Bibliography is consciously placed in service to build socialism and communism and directed toward satisfying the variety of informational needs of the Soviet people -- the builders of communism, who are totally subordinate to these sublime goals." During the First All-Russian bibliographic conference in 1924, Tropovskii was already promoting the recommendatory, propagandistic bibliography in his paper "O sviazi teoreticheskoi i prakticheskoi bibliografii." The pre-revolutionary bibliographic traditions and their followers, for whom bibliographic objectivity and scholarly values were dominant, were still relatively strong, and Tropovskii and his peers, such as I.P. Grebenshchikov, I.B. Simanovskii, and M.N. Kufaev remained without much influence. The situation, however, changed drastically during the second conference in 1926, orchestrated by Nadezhda Krupskaia. During it Tropovskii introduced and imposed on the profession the concept of "partiinost' bibliografii." Service oriented, recommendatory bibliography became the official mandate, and it influenced bibliographic work for at least quarter of a century.

These tendencies are evident when one examines the bibliographic works. In the 1920's Mez'er's important bibliography: SLOVARNYI UKAZATEL' PO KNIGOVEDENIIU (1924) could be published, and B.S. Bodnarskii and N.I. Matsuev, through individual efforts, produced current bibliographies: the former, BIBLIOGRAFIIA RUSSKOI BIBLIOGRAFII, and the latter, KHUDOZHESTVENNAIA LITERATURA RUSSKAIA I PEREVODNAIA. In the early 1930's there appeared A.G. Fomin, PUTEVODITEL' PO BIBLIOGRAFII, BIOBIBLIOGRAFII, ISTORIOGRAFII, KHRONOLOGII I ENTSIKLOPEDII LITERATURY...1736-1932 (1934). In later years, however, bibliographies covering pre-Revolutionary literature or Western imprints disappear almost entirely. Theoretical works were already being written under the new principle of partiinost', for example, the first textbook on bibliography, E.I. Shamurin's METODIKA BIBLIOGRAFICHESKOI RABOTY (1933); N.V. Zdobnov's ISTORIIA RUSSKOI BIBLIOGRAFII (1st ed. 1944-1947, 2nd ed. 1951); and works by I.N. Rozanov, V.I. Nevskii, M.N. Kufaev and others. In the 1940's Stalinism, war, and economic hardship all contributed to a standstill in bibliographic production.

Toward the end of the decade the Social Science Library at the Academy of Sciences (Fundamental'naia Biblioteka po Obshchestvennym Naukam [FBON]) initiated current registration of Soviet and international literature in the humanities and social sciences in monthly issues of the bibliographic bulletins NOVAIA SOVETSKAIA I INOSTRANNAIA LITERATURA PO... These bulletins were not distributed commercially.

The post-Stalin era brings a "revolution" in

bibliography. Although both institutes of culture were still dominated by hard-line theoreticians, in Moscow by A.D. Eikhengol'ts and in Leningrad by Mikhail A. Briskman, a change begins to take shape. This is evident in the textbook prepared by the leading theoreticians and bibliographers B.Ia. Bukhshtab et al. (part 1) and E.I. Ryskin et al. (part 2); BIBLIOGRAFIIA KHUDOZHESTVENNOI LITERATURY I LITERATUROVEDENIIA (Moscow, Part 1, 1960, Part 2, 1950). On one hand, Bukhshtab writes in the introduction that by using the Communist partiinost' principle as a starting point, Soviet bibliography serves "as a serious weapon of propaganda and communist education. By selecting literature according to Marxist-Leninist ideology, systematizing and actively recommending it in response to the needs of various groups of readers, bibliography helps the Soviet people in their creative, constructive efforts to promote the cultural growth of the nation." He orients his textbook accordingly by devoting much more attention to recommendatory than to scholarly bibliographies. On the other hand, a major part of Ryskin's presentation (part 2), which is more practical in scope, deals primarily with scholarly bibliography with less ideological bias.

The 1950's were ripe for major works. In the history of bibliography, the series DEIATELI KNIGI provided biographies of major bibliographers. After Zdobnov's death Bodnarskii edited both his history of bibliography (3rd ed. 1955) and SINKHRONICHESKIE TABLITSY RUSSKOI BIBLIOGRAFII, 1700-1928 SO SPISKOM VAZHNEISHIKH BIBLIOGRAFICHESKIKH TRUDOV. MATERIALY DLIA ISTORII RUSSKOI BIBLIOGRAFII (Moscow, VKP, 1962), the latter already prepared in 1928. Pre-revolutionary works in bibliography were listed in M.V. Sokurova, OBSHCHIE BIBLIOGRAFII RUSSKIKH KNIG GRAZHDANSKOI PECHATI (1956); M.V. Sokurova, M.V. Mashkova, OBSHCHIE BIBLIOGRAFII RUSSKIKH PERIODICHESKIKH IZDANII (1956); I.M. Kaufman's monumental RUSSKIE BIOGRAFICHESKIE I BIOBIBLIOGRAFICHESKIE SLOVARI (1955); SVODNYI KATALOG RUSSKOI KNIGI XVIII VEKA (1955 and continuation through the 1970's); BIBLIOGRAFIIA RUSSKOI BIBLIOGRAFII PO ISTORII SSSR. ANNOTIROVANNYI PERECHEN' BIBLIOGRAFICHESKIKH UKAZATELEI, IZDANNYKH DO 1917 GODA (1957). Major retrospective registration of Soviet imprints began with ISTORIIA SSSR. UKAZATEL' SOVETSKOI LITERATURY ZA 1917-1952 GG. (1956-). In the 1960's substantial bibliographic works covered the whole spectrum of Russian literature: R.P. Dmitrieva dealt with the Chronicles (LETOPISI, 1962); N.F. Droblenkova with the eleventh to seventeenth centuries, (1961); V.P. Stepanov, Iu.V. Stennik with the eighteenth century (1968), K.D. Muratova with the nineteenth century (1963), and the end of nineteenth and beginning of the 20th centuries (1963). All these bibliographies were sponsored by the Academy of Sciences Pushkinskii Dom. At the same time, the Saltykov-Shchedrin Public Library in Leningrad sponsored RUSSKIE SOVETSKIE PISATELI. PROZAIKI (1959-1972).

In history there appeared a guide: A.L. Shapiro's BIBLIOGRAFIIA ISTORII SSSR (1968), a bibliography of bibliographies: ISTORIIA SSSR. ANNOTIROVANNYI PERECHEN' RUSSKIKH BIBLIOGRAFII, IZDANNYKH DO 1965 G. (1966), and ISTORIIA ISTORICHESKOI NAUKI V SSSR, DOOKTIABR'SKII PERIOD. BIBLIOGRAFIIA (1965). In nineteenth-century Russian linguistics, BIBLIOGRAFICHESKII UKAZATEL' LITERATURY PO RUSSKOMU IAZYKOZNANIIU S 1825 PO 1880 GOD (1954-1959) and a bibliography of bibliographies BIBLIOGRAFIIA BIBLIOGRAFII PO IAZYKOZNANIIU. ANNOTIROVANNYI SISTEMATICHESKII UKAZATEL' OTECHESTVENNYKH IZDANII (1963) were published. Even F.A. Shibanov's UKAZATEL' KARTOGRAFICHESKOI LITERATURY, VYSHEDSHEI V ROSSII S 1800 PO 1917 GOD (1961) is indicative of the departure from the focus on Soviet imprints alone and recommendatory standards, and the move toward universal and scholarly qualities. The new atmosphere and the improvement in economic conditions led to the development of expensively produced current bibliographies such as BIBLIOGRAFIIA IZDANII AKADEMII NAUK SSSR. EZHEGODNIK (1956-); SOVETSKOE LITERATUROVEDENIE I KRITIKA. RUSSKAIA SOVETSKAIA LITERATURA... (1966-); SLAVIANSKOE IAZYKOZNANIE. BIBLIOGRAFICHESKII UKAZATEL' LITERATURY, IZDANNOI V SSSR S... (1963-); and others, published in journals and elsewhere. Guides to archives were also issued, some were general: GOSUDARSTVENNYE ARKHIVY SOIUZA SSR. KRATKII SPRAVOCHNIK edited by G.A. Belov (1956), LICHNYE ARKHIVNYE FONDY V GOSUDARSTVENNYKH KHRANILISHCHAKH SSSR (1962), others pertained to individual archives. All these works facilitated the serious study of Russian culture in a fashion unprecedented for the Soviet period.

This momentum continued to the middle of the 1970's. The 1970's can be typified by such works as SPRAVOCHNIKI PO ISTORII DOREVOLIUTSIONNOI ROSSII (1971); or ISTORIIA DOREVOLIUTSIONNOI ROSSII V DNEVNIKAKH I VOSPOMINANIAKH... (1976-): works which could hardly be published during the period of Stalin's domination. To this tradition also belong VOSPOMINANIIA I DNEVNIKI, UKAZATEL' RUKOPISEI XVIII-XX VV. (1976); B.L. Kandel', RUSSKAIA KHUDOZHESTVENNAIA LITERATURA I LITERATUROVEDENIE (1976); and Iu.I. Masanov, UKAZATELI SODERZHANIIA RUSSKIKH ZHURNALOV I PRODOLZHAIUSHCHIKHSIA IZDANII, 1755-1970 GG. (1975).

During the second part of the 1970's theoretical questions of bibliography have attracted more attention, especially in works by A.I. Barsuk, O.P. Korshunov, or Iu.M. Laufer in literary bibliography (TEORIIA I METODIKA SOVETSKOI LITERATURNOI BIBLIOGRAFII. Moscow, Kniga, 1978). The impact on bibliographic practice of these theoretical works is not yet visible. It appears, however, that coverage of pre-revolutionary works has been scaled down and restricted to more specialized bibliographies. The scene is dominated by the activity of the Institut Nauchnoi Informatsii po Obshchestvennym Naukam in Moscow, which focuses on current and retrospective bibliographic registration beginning with 1917 imprints. The Saltykov-Shchedrin Public Library in Leningrad stresses Soviet literature. Its major ongoing project is the sequel to RUSSKIE SOVETSKIE PISATELI. PROZAIKI (1959-1972), namely RUSSKIE SOVETSKIE PISATELI. POETY (1977-). On the other hand, libraries across the country have intensified the publication of catalogs of their manuscripts and rare materials. An interesting development along these lines is the publication of a multivolume, worldwide project SVODNYI KATALOG I OPISANIE STAROPECHATNYKH IZDANII KIRILLOVSKOGO I GLAGOLICHESKOGO SHRIFTOV, which began in 1979.

Today the "recommendatory" bibliography has reentered the Soviet scene with renewed vigor. The All-Union conference "The Role of Recommendatory Bibliography in Communist Education and in the Scientific-Technological Process" was held in Moscow September 19-21, 1983. The keynote address by the newly appointed director of the Lenin Public Library in Moscow, N.S. Kartashov, "Vospitanie novogo cheloveka i rekomendatel'naia bibliografiia" (Education of the New Man and Recommendatory Bibliography), published in SOVETSKAIA BIBLIOGRAFIIA 1,1984:3-19, set the tone for the proceedings. The conference intended to translate into their bibliographic reality the directives of the Party Plenum held in June 1983. Thus bibliographic forces have been gathered around the communist doctrinal, political, and educational objectives, and to repudiate capitalism and its philosophy. This, then, seems to be the focus of bibliography during the Andropov/Chernenko era. How much elbowroom will remain for research bibliography, coverage of Western publications in Soviet bibliographies, broadness and objectivity, is yet to be seen. It may be added that the Third All Union Conference of the Library Soviet at the Ministry of Culture, held September 12-13, 1983, promoted similar educational standards by stating, for example: "It is mandatory to employ the most effective tools which will actively influence the formation of Marxist-Leninist ideology; to devote major attention to preparation and publication of bibliographies (posobii) which foster planned and multifaceted development of advanced socialism..." (trans. by W.Z. from "Plenum Vsesoiuznogo bibliotechnogo Soveta," SOVETSKAIA BIBLIOGRAFIIA 1,1984:81). It seems, therefore, that the 1980's will have their own bibliographic guiding principles and profile.

The advent of automation as applied to bibliographic services has been slow in the Soviet Union. International bibliographic cooperation with the West is very limited. As a consequence, Soviet scholarship is inadequately represented in Western bibliographies available through computerized facilities. Thus the scholar and bibliographer will have to rely on printed bibliographies for some time to come. Nevertheless, Western bibliographic sources such as computerized library networks and major bibliographic services available both in computerized and printed form such as the SOCIAL SCIENCE CITATION INDEX, ARTS AND HUMANITIES CITATION INDEX, MLA INTERNATIONAL BIBLIOGRAPHY OF BOOKS AND ARTICLES ON THE MODERN LANGUAGES AND LITERATURES are including more Russian language entries every year and should not be overlooked as useful bibliographic sources. These, however, are outside the scope of this work.

3. Libraries, archives, museums

3.1. Libraries

Libraries help to shape the concept of bibliography. While American librarians and libraries have devoted their largest effort to elaborate cataloging schemes, comparable effort in the Soviet Union has been devoted to compiling bibliographies as access to information. (Soviet libraries, being closed-stack libraries, do not provide direct access to materials. Perhaps the open versus closed stack practice has had some influence on shaping this difference between cataloging and bibliographic orientation.) All major Soviet libraries have departments which produce bibliographies. Their role is central to our understanding of the whole bibliographic network, including the quality, bibliographic standards, and physical format of their products. The bibliographic responsibilities for different subject areas are assigned to various libraries. (See history of Soviet bibliography, above.)

Besides bibliographic functions, libraries provide access to collections. Effective use of them depends in part on knowledge of a particular library's history, operations, and facilities, as well as available catalogs and other information tools. Users of Soviet libraries should remember that many of them lack historical continuity due to war and revolution. Libraries experienced forced reorganization, centralization, and the redistribution of library and archival holdings. As a result, many of the older pre-1917 library directories, guides, and catalogs have only historical value.

3.1.1. Histories of libraries

Soviet scholars have yet to produce the definitive history of libraries in the Soviet Union. The following textbooks have been published:

Vasil'chenko, V.I. OCHERK ISTORII BIBLIOTECHNOGO DELA V ROSSII XI-XVIII VV. Moscow, Gos. izd. kul'turno-prosvetitel'noi literatury, 1948.

Abramov, K.I., Vasil'chenko, V.I. ISTORIIA BIBLIOTECHNOGO DELA V SSSR (DO 1917 G.). Moscow, Sovetskaia Rossiia, 1959.

Vasil'chenko, V.I. ISTORIIA BIBLIOTECHNOGO DELA V SSSR. UCHEBNIK DLIA BIBLIOTECHNYKH INSTITUTOV. Moscow, Sovetskaia Rossiia, 1958.

Abramov, K.I. ISTORIIA BIBLIOTECHNOGO DELA V SSSR. Moscow, Sovetskaia Rossiia, 1959; 2nd ed. Moscow, Kniga, 1970; 3rd ed. Moscow, Kniga, 1980.

Research on the history of libraries is extensive, although surveys are not many. Histories of libraries are also included in works on the history of books and publishing by such writers as S.P. Luppov (see above 1.1). Research on pre-revolutionary libraries includes:

Slukhovskii, M.I. BIBLIOTECHNOE DELO V ROSSII DO XVIII VEKA: IZ ISTORII KNIZHNOGO PROSVESHCHENIIA. Moscow, Kniga, 1968.

Slukhovskii, M.I. RUSSKAIA BIBLIOTEKA XVI-XVII VV. Moscow, Kniga, 1973.

and for the Soviet period:

Abramov, K.I. BIBLIOTECHNOE STROITEL'STVO V PERVYE GODY SOVETSKOI VLASTI. Moscow, Kniga, 1974.

Abramov, K.I. BIBLIOTECHNOE STROITEL'STVO V SSSR 1917-1977 GG. Moscow, Kniga, 1977.

ISTORIIA BIBLIOTECHNOGO DELA V SSSR. DOKUMENTY I MATERIALY, 1918-1920. K.I. Abramov, ed. Moscow, Kniga, 1975.

ISTORIIA BIBLIOTECHNOGO DELA V SSSR. DOKUMENTY I MATERIALY, NOIABR' 1920-1929 GG. K.I. Abramov, ed. Moscow, Kniga, 1979.

There are, however, good histories of individual libraries, and a listing of these works can be found in the newly published KNIGOVEDENIE. ENTSIKLOPEDICHESKII SLOVAR', mentioned above. Unfortunately, this source lists only a few pre-revolutionary studies. For those the researcher should consult Mez'er's SLOVARNYI UKAZATEL' PO KNIGOVEDENIIU, 1924 ed., pp. 59-111 and 1931 ed., vol. 1, pp. 144-303.

An example of a recent work in this area is E.I. Lesokhina, A.M. Khar'kova, ISTORIIA BIBLIOTEKI MOSKOVSKOGO UNIVERSITETA (Moscow, Universitet, 1981) which continues work done by N.A. Penchko discussing the history of the Moscow University Library up to 1812 (Moscow, Universitet, 1969); and work by V.V. Sorokin for the period 1800-1917 (Moscow, Universitet, 1980).

The Soviet ideologist in the area of library science is:

A.N. Vaneev, RAZVITIE BIBLIOTEKOVEDCHESKOI MYSLI V SSSR. Moscow, Kniga, 1980.

The leading journal dealing with the theory of librarianship and the history of libraries is SOVETSKOE BIBLIOTEKOVEDENIE. NAUCHNYI SBORNIK (1973-, 6 issues per year), which supersedes BIBLIOTEKI SSSR (1950-1973). Here one finds, for example, a survey of research activities, "Soderzhanie i organizatsiia issledovanii (k pervym itogam za 10 let)" by L.M. In'kova and I.P. Osipova (2, 1981:4-23, with extensive bibliographic footnotes); and a chronological outline of major developments and legal documents pertaining to Soviet libraries, "Bibliotechnaia zhizn' Soiuza SSR (1922-1982)" (4,1982:40-49).

Prolific research in the history of libraries and librarianship is conducted by the leading Soviet libraries. The Saltykov-Shchedrin Public Library in Leningrad publishes collections of scholarly papers, formerly issued as SBORNIK (vols. 1-3, 1953-1955) and TRUDY (vols. 1-12, 1957-1964). The corresponding serial of the Lenin Public Library in Moscow is TRUDY (1,1957-), but note should also be taken of its more focused ISTORIIA BIBLIOTECHNOGO DELA V SSSR. SBORNIK NAUCHNYKH TRUDOV. Vol. III of the latter, which is entitled ISTOCHNIKOVEDCHESKIE PROBLEMY ISTORII BIBLIOTECHNOGO DELA V SSSR (1912-1929) (Moscow, [MPB], 1977) contains A.N. Vaneev's article "Istochniki po istorii bibliotekovedcheskoi mysli v SSSR" (pp.80-98). Vaneev stresses the political principles guiding the development of Soviet libraries. The activities of this Library, its publishing and bibliographic work, and a staff directory are recorded in GOSUDARSTVENNAIA ORDENA LENINA BIBLIOTEKA SSSR IMENI V.I. LENINA V... GODU (a similar publication issued by the Saltykov-Shchedrin library in Leningrad has been discontinued) and "Spisok pechatnykh katalogov, otrazhaiushchikh fondy Gosudarstvennoi biblioteki SSSR imeni V.I. Lenina" in TRUDY Vol. 16, 1980:178-181. Serial publications are also issued by the two leading Institutes of Culture (Gosudarstvennyi bibliotechnyi institut), one in Moscow which publishes UCHENYE ZAPISKI (1955-), and the other in Leningrad publishing TRUDY (1956-). The Soviet Academy of Sciences Library irregularly publishes BIBLIOTEKI AKADEMII NAUK SSSR I AKADEMII SOIUZNYKH RESPUBLIK. SBORNIK NAUCHNYKH TRUDOV (Vyp. 1: IZ ISTORII BIBLIOTECHNOGO DELA I BIBLIOGRAFII (Leningrad, 1978). This supersedes BIBLIOTECHNO-BIBLIOGRAFICHESKAIA INFORMATSIIA BIBLIOTEK AKADEMII NAUK SSSR I SOIUZNYKH BIBLIOTEK (1956-1973) and BIBLIOTEKI AKADEMII NAUK SSSR I AKADEMII NAUK SOIUZNYKH RESPUBLIK (4 issues annually, 1974-1977). Its publishing activities have been recorded by G.V. Sergienko, BIBLIOTEKA AKADEMII NAUK SSSR. UKAZATEL' LITERATURY ZA 1964-1974 GG. (Leningrad, BAN, 1981). This work continues BIBLIOTEKA AKADEMII NAUK SSSR. 1714-1964. BIBLIOGRAFICHESKII UKAZATEL' (Leningrad, BAN, 1964).

The research and bibliographic activities of the Siberian Branch of the Academy of Sciences in Novosibirsk are also important. Information about them is provided by P. Polansky, "The bibliographic work of the State Public Scientific-Technical Library of the Siberian Section of the USSR Academy of Sciences", LIBRI 4,1983:274-288.

3.1.2. Bibliography on libraries and librarianship

Current bibliographic listings in this field are to be found in BIBLIOTEKOVEDENIE I BIBLIOGRAFIIA SSSR (1974-, monthly) which supersedes BIBLIOTEKOVEDENIE I BIBLIOGRAFIIA. UKAZATEL' SOVETSKOI LITERATURY (1963-1973, monthly). N.S. Trishkina has prepared BIBLIOGRAFICHESKAIA RABOTA BIBLIOTEK SOVETSKOGO

SOIUZA. UKAZATEL' KNIG I STATEI NA RUSSKOM IAZYKE ZA 1972-1980 GG. (Moscow, 1981). Some bibliographic references on the history of libraries may be found in an annual listing by L.I. Fursenko in KNIGA. ISSLEDOVANIIA I MATERIALY; F. Krause, et al., BIBLIOTHEKSWESEN UND BIBLIOGRAPHIE (Leipzig, Bibliographisches Institut VEB, 1978); D.B. Grechushnikova, et al., GOSUDARSTVENNYE BIBLIOTEKI SOIUZNYKH RESPUBLIK. UKAZATEL' LITERATURY. 1967-1982 GG. (Moscow, 1982); and Z.I. Kolchinina, OSNOVNYE POKAZATELI GOSUDARSTVENNYKH BIBLIOTEK SOIUZNYKH RESPUBLIK ZA 1976-1980 GG. (Moscow, 1982).

3.1.3. Library catalogs

3.1.3.1. General

The printed catalog of a large library can be a useful place to start a bibliographic search, especially when the catalog includes subject access. The use of catalogs is further enhanced by progressive development of catalogs on line. But under no circumstances can a library catalog, whether in card form or on line, substitute for a bibliography. This is due to the relatively limited options used in assigning catalog subject headings, the frequent lack of analytics of monographic series, cataloging inconsistencies usually resulting from the historical development of cataloging theory and practice, limited library resources which may not hold the crucial materials on the subject under research, and the exclusion of periodical literature from catalogs. Catalogs of large libraries can identify major bibliographies and monographs, and are helpful in bibliographic verification of data. As such their bibliogra-phic value cannot be disregarded.

A particularly useful category of catalogs are the union catalogs (svodnye katalogi), which incorporate the holdings of several libraries. For American scholars such a source is the SLAVIC CYRILLIC UNION CATALOG FOR PRE-1956 IMPRINTS (Totowa, N.J., Rowman & Littlefield, 1980. Microfiche). It includes pre-1956 Cyrillic alphabet imprints reported to the Library of Congress by the American libraries up to 1979. It supersedes the

CYRILLIC UNION CATALOG (New York, Readex Co., 1952. Microcard). For Russian/Soviet and East European imprints, including non-Cyrillic alphabets, one can consult THE NATIONAL UNION CATALOG (publishers vary, the most recent is Washington, D.C., The Library of Congress) published since 1983 on microfiche.

Among the most prominent American libraries that have Slavic research collections and published catalogs are: Harvard University, The Hoover Institution on War, Revolution, and Peace, the University of California, Berkeley, and the New York Public Library. The latter is especially useful for detecting monographs in series.

Printed catalogs of libraries outside the United States are listed by J.S.G. Simmons, RUSSIAN BIBLIOGRAPHY... (cited below), pp.4-14 (including archives). Of note among them are the catalogs of the Helsinki University Library, available on microfilm in some United States libraries, e.g., at the University of Illinois at Urbana-Champaign and the Hoover Institution at Stanford; and the Leningrad University Library: KATALOG RUSSKIKH KNIG BIBLIOTEKI IMP. S.-PETERBURGSKOGO UNIVERSITETA (St. Petersburg, 1897-1902. 2 vols). Both are bibliographically important, on the one hand as catalogs of depository libraries, and on the other because there are no comprehensive bibliographies of Russian imprints covering the nineteenth century up to 1917.

In the Soviet Union printed library catalogs of entire collections are uncommon. What are produced are union catalogs (svodnye katalogi). They are arranged much like a bibliography: usually chronologically, with author, title, subject, and geographic indexes. Thus, despite their name "katalog", they are actually bibliographies with an indication of the location of the listed items. This genre of catalog covers imprints from the beginning of printing in Russia (1553) to the end of the eighteenth century. The union catalog of manuscript books is in preparation. The first volume of this project has appeared in 1984. These and early imprints are listed in the plethora of special catalogs produced by different libraries listing their own holdings. As such they are the primary bibliographic sources for both manuscripts and early imprints. Information about existing printed catalogs can be obtained from bibliographies of bibliographies and sections below.

3.1.3.2. Manuscript books

Catalogs of manuscript collections are published by Soviet libraries across the country, old and new, large and small. Libraries in Russia have had a tumultuous history, thus it is difficult to anticipate which library has manuscript books and whether a printed catalog is available. For textological studies all printed catalogs have value, especially since these catalogs contain information about textological variants, artistic values, the printing, watermarks, etc. Unfortunately, they are typically published in limited editions, and they are seldom distributed commercially. Bibliographies listing these catalogs are now quite dated. The major sources are:

Djaparidze, D. MEDIAEVAL SLAVIC MANUSCRIPTS. A BIBLIOGRAPHY OF PRINTED CATALOGUES. Cambridge, Mass., The Mediaeval Academy of America, 1957. (Mediaeval Academy of America. PUBLICATIONS no. 64).

Rogov, A.I. SVEDENIIA O NEBOL'SHIKH SOBRANIIAKH SLAVIANO-RUSSKIKH RUKOPISEI V SSSR. Moscow, AN SSSR, 1962.

Bel'chikov, N.F., et. al. SPRAVOCHNIK-UKAZATEL' PECHATNYKH OPISANII SLAVIANO-RUSSKIKH RUKOPISEI. Moscow-Leningrad, AN SSSR, 1963.

The union catalog is

SVODNYI KATALOG SLAVIANO-RUSSKIKH RUKOPISNYKH KNIG, KHRANIASHCHIKHSIA V SSSR. XI-XIII VV. Moscow, Nauka, 1984. Volumes for later centuries are in preparation, see introduction to this work.

Manuscript catalogs such as OPISANIE RUKOPISNOGO OTDELA BIBLIOTEKI AKADEMII NAUK SSSR (St. Petersburg, 1910. 2 vols. continued in Leningrad, 1959-), RUKOPISNYE SOBRANIIA GOSUDARSTVENNOI BIBLIOTEKI SSSR IMENI V. I. LENINA. UKAZATEL' (Moscow, 1983- Tom 1. Vyp. 1: 1862-1917), and P.K. Grimsted bibliographies on archives contain information about manuscript books as well as non book manuscripts. Consult section on archives.

3.1.3.3. Imprints up to 1800

New catalogs to individual collections of early Russian imprints are published every year. There is no readily available bibliography listing them. However, catalogs to major collections and union catalogs listed below will provide adequate information about titles published up to 1800. The major work is:

SVODNYI KATALOG I OPISANIE STAROPECHATNYKH IZDANII KIRILLOVSKOGO I GLAGOLICHESKOGO SHRIFTOV. Moscow, [MPB], 1979-

Until this work is finished useful information can be found in:

V POMOSHCH' SOSTAVITELIAM SVODNOGO KATALOGA STAROPECHATNYKH IZDANII KIRILLOVSKOGO I GLAGOLICHESKOGO SHRIFTOV. Moscow, [MPB], 1976.

Pozdeeva, V.I., et al. KATALOG KNIG KIRILLICHESKOI PECHATI XV-XVII VV. NAUCHNOI BIBLIOTEKI MOSKOVSKOGO UNIVERSITETA. Moscow, Universitet, 1980.

Zernova, A.S. KNIGI KIRILLOVSKOI PECHATI IZDANNYE V MOSKVE V XVI-XVII VV. SVODNYI KATALOG. Moscow, [MPB], 1958.

Zernova, A.S. SVODNYI KATALOG RUSSKOI KNIGI KIRILLOVSKOI PECHATI XVIII V. Moscow, [MPB], 1968.

Bykova, T.A., et al. OPISANIE IZDANII, NAPECHATANNYKH PRI PETRE I. SVODNYI KATALOG. It consists of three independent titles:

OPISANIE IZDANII, NAPECHATANNYKH KIRILLITSEI, 1689-IAN. 1725. Moscow-Leningrad, AN SSSR, 1958.

OPISANIE IZDANII GRAZHANSKOI PECHATI, 1709- IAN. 1725. Moscow-Leningrad, AN SSSR, 1955.

DOPOLNENIIA I PRILOZHENIIA. Leningrad, AN SSSR, 1972. (Supplement to both works).

SVODNYI KATALOG RUSSKOI KNIGI GRAZHDANSKOI PECHATI XVIII V., 1725-1800. Moscow, 1962-67, 5 vols., and Supplement, 1975.

rev.: N. Kochetkova, AN SSSR, IZVESTIIA, SERIIA LITERATURY I IAZYKA, t. 27, vyp., 6, pp. 560-561.
V.P. Stepanov, RUSSKAIA LITERATURA, 3, 1969: 248-49.
V.A. Zapadov, "Bibliografiia i archivy", RUSSKAIA LITERATURA, 1969: 207-213.
M. Polonskaia, "Itogi raboty po sostavleniiu Svodnogo...", Moscow. Publichnaia biblioteka. TRUDY. Tom XI, 1969:126-144.

SVODNYI KATALOG KNIG NA INOSTRANNYKH IAZYKAKH, IZDANNYKH V ROSSII V XVIII V. 1701-1800. Leningrad, Nauka, 1984-

3.1.3.4. Private collections

Several catalogs to private collections are bibliographically important. For information about them see: RUSSKIE BIBLIOTEKI I CHASTNYE KNIZHNYE SOBRANIIA XVI-XIX VEKOV. SBORNIK NAUCHNYKH TRUDOV. Leningrad. BAN, 1979. Russia has had numerous private collectors whose collections are preserved as entities in major Soviet libraries. Information about manuscript book collections can be found in works by P.K. Grimsted (see below). As an example of such a collection see:

Titov, A. OPISANIE SLAVIANO-RUSSKIKH RUKOPISEI... St. Petersburg - Moscow, 1893-1913, 6 vols.

Bibliographies - catalogs of general bibliographic importance are:

Ul'ianinskii, D.V. BIBLIOTEKA D.V. UL'IANINSKOGO. Moscow, 1912-1915. 3 vols. Vol. 2 is especially valuable as bibliography of bibliographies.

Smirnov-Sokol'skii, N.O. MOIA BIBLIOTEKA. BIBLIOGRAFICHESKOE OPISANIE. Moscow, Kniga, 1969. 2 vols. (extensive annotations).

Both libraries are presently housed in the Lenin Public Library in Moscow. Catalogs of major private collections are listed in general bibliographies (see Part I. 4.3).

3.1.3.5. Periodical collections

Russian/Soviet serials have comprehensive bibliographies. These are discussed in a separate section. The catalogs of periodical collections have the practical purpose of locating titles rather than of identifying them bibliographically.

The most important library catalogs are:

In the United States:

UNION LIST OF SERIALS with coverage up to 1950,

continued by NEW SERIAL TITLES.

HALF A CENTURY OF SOVIET SERIALS, 1917-1968. A BIBLIOGRAPHY AND UNION LIST OF SERIALS PUBLISHEI IN THE USSR. Washington, D.C., Library of Congress, 1968, 2 vols.

Hoskins, J.W. THE USSR AND EAST CENTRAL AND SOUTH-EASTERN EUROPE: PERIODICALS IN WESTERN LANGUAGES. Washington, D.C., Library of Congress, 1980.

Russian émigré catalogs:

Bakunina, T.A. L'ÉMIGRATION RUSSE EN EUROPE. CATALOGUE COLLECTIF DES PERIODIQUES EN LANGUE RUSSE, 1855-1940. Paris, Institut d'Études Slaves, 1976 (Bibliothèque Russe de l'Institut d'Études Slaves, Tom XL/1).

Volkoff, A.-M. same title, 1940-1970. Same publisher 1977 (same series, Tome XL/2).

The most important Soviet catalogs:

ALFAVITNYI SLUZHEBNYI KATALOG RUSSKIKH DOREVOLIU-TSIONNYKH GAZET (1703-1916). Leningrad, SS, 1958.

Nizheva, O.N., et al., eds. RUSSKIE DOREVOLIUTSION-NYE GAZETY V FONDAKH GOS. BIBLIOTEKI SSSR IM. V.I. LENINA, 1702-1916; ALFAVITNYI KATALOG. Moscow, MPB, 1977. 2 parts.

KATALOG PERIODICHESKIKH IZDANII NA RUSSKOM IAZYKE NAUCHNOI BIBLIOTEKI MOSKOVSKOGO UNIVERSITETA (PO SOSTOIANIIU NA 1 IANVARIA 1974). ZHURNALY. BIBLIOGRAFICHESKII UKAZATEL'. Moscow, Universitet, Tom 1, 1976-

Garshina, N.A. KATALOG OTECHESTVENNYKH ZHURNALOV NA RUSSKOM IAZYKE NA 1917-1977 GG., KHRANIASHCHIKHSIA V FONDAKH GPIB. [GOS. PUBLICHNOI ISTORICHESKOI BIBLIOTEKI]. Moscow, 1981.

3.1.4. Directories of libraries

BIBLIOTEKI SSSR. SPRAVOCHNIK:
- BIBLIOTEKI RSFSR. Moscow, Kniga, 1974;
- BIBLIOTEKI SOIUZNYKH RESPUBLIK (BEZ RSFSR). Moscow, Kniga, 1973;
- BIBLIOTEKI SSSR OBSHCHESTVENNO-POLITICHESKOGO, FILOLOGICHESKOGO I ISKUSTVOVEDCHESKOGO PROFILIA. Moscow, Kniga, 1969.

BIBLIOTEKI AKADEMII NAUK SSSR. SPRAVOCHNIK. Moscow, Kniga, 1959.

In addition to these there are directories to libraries in major cities, e.g.,

BIBLIOTEKI MOSKVY. SPRAVOCHNIK. Moscow, Kniga, 1979.

BIBLIOTEKI LENINGRADA. SPRAVOCHNIK. Moscow, Kniga, 1965.

Laskeev, N.A. SPRAVOCHNIK-PUTEVODITEL' PO SETI SPETSIAL'NYKH BIBLIOTEK AKADEMICHESKIKH UCHREZHDENII. Leningrad, BAN, 1983.

3.2. Archives

3.2.1. Literature about archives

As in the case of manuscript books, non-book manuscripts are not registered in general bibliographies. Manuscripts are deposited both in the archives and in manuscript sections of libraries. Bibliographic access to them is provided through published and unpublished inventories, descriptions, and guides. Very often the history of an archive or library, or a report on previous research based on their holdings, may offer clues to collections. Nevertheless, manuscripts are the most difficult area for bibliographic investigation.

History of archives (see also guides to archives 3.2.2.):

Ikonnikov, V.S. OPYT RUSSKOI ISTORIOGRAFII. Kiev, Universitet, 1891. Vol. 1, pp. 377-1539.

Maiakovskii, I.L. OCHERKI PO ISTORII ARKHIVNOGO DELA V SSSR. 2nd ed. Moscow, Glavnoe Arkhivnoe Upravlenie NKVD SSSR, 1960. Vol. 1 (for pre-revolutionary Russia).

Maksakov, V.V. ISTORIIA I ORGANIZATSIIA ARKHIVNOGO DELA V SSSR. 1917-1945. Moscow, Nauka, 1969.

Vialikov, V.I. ARKHIVNOE STROITEL'STVO V SSSR. 1946-1967 GG. UCHEBNOE POSOBIE. Moscow, 1972.

Belov, G.A. ZUR GESCHICHTE, THEORIE UND PRAXIS DES ARCHIVWESENS IN DER UDSSR. Marburg, Archivschule, 1971.

Bibliography:

SOVETSKAIA ARKHEOGRAFIIA. ANNOTIROVANNYI KATALOG NAUCHNO-METODICHESKOI LITERATURY. 1917-1970 GG. Moscow, Glavnoe Arkhivnoe Upravlenie, (GAU), 1974, Vol. 1.

See also:

KATALOG ARKHIVOVEDCHESKOI LITERATURY I SBORNIKOV DOKUMENTOV. 1960-1963. Moscow, GAU, 1964 and for 1964-1967. Moscow, GAU, 1970;

KATALOG SBORNIKOV DOKUMENTOV. 1917-1960. Moscow, GAU, 1961;

KATALOG ARKHIVOVEDCHESKOI LITERATURY. 1917-1959. Moscow, GAU, 1961;

ARKHEOGRAFICHESKII EZHEGODNIK, 1957-

The leading journal is

SOVETSKIE ARKHIVY, 1966- six times a year; it supersedes VOPROSY ARKHIVOVEDENIIA, 1959-1965, quarterly; and ARKHIVNOE DELO, 1923-1941, 58 issues, irregular.

3.2.2. General guides and textbooks

Major guides to archives will usually provide the historical background, a bibliography on archival literature in general as well as on a specific archive, some directory data, and a general description of holdings. The most important sources in this category are:

Grossman, Iu.M., Kutik, V.N. SPRAVOCHNIK NAUCHNOGO RABOTNIKA. ARKHIVY, DOKUMENTY, ISSLEDOVATEL'. 2nd rev. ed. L'vov, Universitet, 1983. (1st ed., 1979).

Belov, G.A., ed. GOSUDARSTVENNYE ARKHIVY SOIUZA SSSR. KRATKII SPRAVOCHNIK. Moscow, GAU, 1956.

Levshin, B.V., ed. KRATKII SPRAVOCHNIK PO NAUCHNO-OTRASLEVYM I MEMORIAL'NYM ARKHIVAM AN SSSR. Moscow, Nauka, 1979.

Grimsted, P.K. ARCHIVES AND MANUSCRIPT REPOSITORIES IN THE USSR: MOSCOW AND LENINGRAD. Princeton, Princeton University Press, 1972.
SUPPLEMENT 1. Zug, Inter Documentation Co., 1976.

Grimsted, P.K. "Regional state archives in the USSR: Some notes and bibliography of published guides", SLAVIC REVIEW 1,1969:92-115.

Grimsted, P.K. ARCHIVES AND MANUSCRIPT REPOSITORIES IN THE USSR: ESTONIA, LATVIA, LITHUANIA, BELO-RUSSIA. Princeton, Princeton University Press, 1981.

Grimsted, P.K. "Recent publications on archives and manuscript collections in the Soviet Union: A selective survey", SLAVIC REVIEW 3,1982:511-533.

Textbooks are:

Gorfein, G.M., Shepelev, L.E. ARKHIVOVEDENIE. UCHEBNOE POSOBIE. Leningrad, Universitet, 1971.

Dremina, G.A. TSENTRAL'NYE GOSUDARSTVENNYE ARKHIVY SSSR. 1945-1970 GG. UCHEBNOE POSOBIE. Moscow, GAU, 1977.

Syrchenko, L.G. LICHNYE FONDY DEIATELEI RUSSKOI LITERATURY I ISKUSSTVA V ARKHIVAKH SSSR. UCHEBNOE POSOBIE. Moscow, 1975.

3.2.3. Lists of archival holdings

Guides describe the contents of libraries and archives and often list published guides to individual archival holdings. There is also a wide range of sources which specifically focus on holdings known most commonly as "putevoditel'" or "opis'". Almost every archive in the Soviet Union has such a catalog of holdings but most of them are not published. Users of Soviet archives, whenever possible, should identify precisely the "fond" or collection they wish to consult through existing bibliographic tools. The bibliographies and guides indicated above will assist them in identifying these works. Examples of specific bibliographic tools are:

To several archives:

LICHNYE ARKHIVNYE FONDY V GOS. KHRANILISHCHAKH SSSR. E.V. Kolosova, ed. Moscow, GAU, 1962. 2 vols. Vol. 3 supplementing earlier volumes was published in 1980.

To one archive (published recently, not listed in Grimsted):

Zaborova, R.B., et al., eds. ANNOTIROVANNYI UKAZATEL' RUKOPISNYKH FONDOV GPB. FONDY RUSSKIKH

DEIATELEI XVIII-XX VV. Leningrad, Gos. Publichnaia Biblioteka im. M.E. Saltykova-Shchedrina, 1981-

RUKOPISNYE SOBRANIIA GOSUDARSTVENNOI BIBLIOTEKI SSSR IMENI V.I. LENINA. UKAZATEL'. Moscow, MPB, 1983-
Tom 1, vyp. 1. 1862-1917. Moscow, MPB, 1983.

Balashova, L.P., et al. VOSPOMINANIIA I DNEVNIKI XVIII-XX VV. UKAZATEL' RUKOPISEI. Moscow, Kniga, 1976. Holdings of the Lenin Public Library in Moscow.

Useful information about archival holdings can be deducted from research conducted in them. Such research reports are registered in:

TEMATIKA ISSLEDOVANII PO DOKUMENTAL'NYM MATERIALAM ARKHIVOV AKADEMII NAUK SSSR. SPRAVOCHNIK. Leningrad, 1,1967- annual.

TEMATIKA ISSLEDOVANII PO DOKUMENTAL'NYM MATERIALAM V TSENTRAL'NYKH GOSUDARSTVENNYKH ARKHIVAKH SSSR. SPRAVOCHNIK. Moscow, 1,1964- annual.

3.3. Guides to Western collections

For extensive listings see:

Simmons, J.S.G. RUSSIAN BIBLIOGRAPHY, LIBRARIES, AND ARCHIVES... Oxford, 1973. (full citation see below 4.2).

Grant, S.A. SCHOLAR'S GUIDE TO WASHINGTON, D.C. RUSSIAN/SOVIET STUDIES. 2nd rev. ed. Washington, D.C., Smithsonian Institution Press, 1984.

Brown, J.H., Grant, S.A. THE RUSSIAN EMPIRE AND THE SOVIET UNION. A GUIDE TO MANUSCRIPT AND ARCHIVAL MATERIALS IN THE UNITED STATES. Boston, G.K. Hall, 1981.

Morely, Ch. "Russian collections in American libraries," GUIDE TO RESEARCH IN RUSSIAN HISTORY. Syracuse, 1951:1-22.

Lewański, R.C. EASTERN EUROPE AND RUSSIA/SOVIET UNION. A HANDBOOK OF WEST EUROPEAN ARCHIVAL AND LIBRARY RESOURCES. New York, Saur, 1980.

Walker, G.P.M., ed. RESOURCES FOR SOVIET, EAST EUROPEAN, AND SLAVONIC STUDIES IN BRITISH LIBRARIES. Birmingham, University of Birmingham, 1981.

Wynar, L.R. SLAVIC ETHNIC LIBARIES, MUSEUMS, AND ARCHIVES IN THE UNITED STATES. A GUIDE AND DIRECTORY. Chicago, American Library Association, 1980.

See also general guides:

THE WORLD OF LEARNING;

WORLD GUIDE TO LIBRARIES, both updated regularly.

3.4. Museums

We do not intend to devote much attention to museums here. However, literature pertaining to museums may have some relevance for work in history, literature, art, etc. For this reason perhaps some rudimentary works may prove helpful:

Ravikovich, D. "Muzeinaia set' RSFSR (Sovremennoe sostoianie)" in Ministerstvo Kul'tury RSFSR. Nauchno-issledovatel'skii institut kul'tury. TRUDY. Vol. 36. MUZEI I SOVREMENNOST'. Vyp.2. Moscow, 1976:33-49.

Bibliography:

Galin, G.A. "Bibliografiia po muzeevedeniiu. 1945-1979 gg.", VOPROSY SOVERSHENSTVOVANIIA MUZEINYKH EKSPOZITSII (OTDEL ISTORII SSSR DOOKTIABR'SKOGO PERIODA). Moscow, 1981:157-163. (TRUDY, 103).

Galin, G.A. "Literaturnye muzei SSSR. Bibliografiia. 1974-1980 gg.", SOVREMENNYE LITERATURNYE MUZEI: NEKOTORYE VOPROSY TEORII I PRAKTIKI. Moscow, 1982. (SBORNIK NAUCHNYKH TRUDOV, 111).

Annual bibliography has been issued by the

Ministerstvo Kul'tury RSFSR. Nauchno-issledovatel'skii Institut Kul'tury in its MUZEINOE DELO V SSSR irregularly since 1971. Beginning with 1974 the current bibliography of works dealing mainly with theory, methodology, and history of museums has been published monthly in

NOVOSTI NAUCHNOI LITERATURY. MUZEEVEDENIE I OKHRANA PAMIATNIKOV. BIBLIOGRAFICHESKAIA INFORMATSIIA, monthly.

Information about museums' holdings can be found in specialized bibliographies, e.g., NOVOSTI NAUCHNOI LITERATURY. IZOBRAZITEL'NOE ISKUSSTVO, published by the same Institute since 1974. The TRUDY (since 1957) of this Institute contained a history of museums.

A specialized but important bibliography is:

Novikova, N.G., ed. IZDANIIA TSENTRAL'NOGO MUZEIA SSSR. 1926-1978 GG. BIBLIOGRAFICHESKII UKAZATEL'. Moscow, 1981.

4. General bibliographies

General bibliographies cover a number of subjects, publishing formats, chronological periods, and geographic regions. They are both bibliographic first-step and touchstone and they allow the researcher to test the thoroughness and reliablity of more specialized bibliographies encountered later on in his/her research. Failure to consult such general works can lead to omissions and, when they are subsequently discovered, extensive, time-consuming backtracking.

There is a network of general bibliographic sources which complement each other as well as draw upon each other. Consequently, there is a degree of repetitiveness which requires knowledge of content, the circumstances under which the bibliographies were compiled, and comprehensiveness. The characteristic features of major bibliographies are outlined in the prefaces of the bibliographies themselves and in histories of bibliographies, textbooks, and guides. Reviews of bibliographies are often helpful. These can be found in SOVETSKAIA BIBLIOGRAFIIA and some other scholarly journals. The bibliographies dealing with book culture listed above will provide retrieval tools for these reviews.

4.1. Textbooks

Textbooks are primarily designated for use in Soviet library schools. In addition to describing major bibliographies, they may outline bibliographic theory, methodology, and history, and discuss bibliographic institutions, types of bibliographic production, and the usefulness of different bibliographies for various groups of readers. In this category should be listed:

Kirpicheva, I.K. BIBLIOGRAFIIA V POMOSHCH' NAUCHNOI RABOTE. METODICHESKOE I SPRAVOCHNOE POSOBIE. Leningrad, [SS], 1958.

continued by

Ienish, E.V. BIBLIOGRAFICHESKII POISK V NAUCHNOI RABOTE. SPRAVOCHNOE POSOBIE-PUTEVODITEL'. Nauchnyi redaktor I.K. Kirpicheva. Moscow, Kniga, 1982.
rev.: M.K. Arkhipova, SB 1,1983:58-61.

Briskman, M.A., Eikhengol'ts, A.D. BIBLIOGRAFIIA. OBSHCHII KURS. Moscow, Kniga, 1969.
An earlier edition is

Eikhengol'ts, A.D. OBSHCHAIA BIBLIOGRAFIIA. UCHEBNIK DLIA BIBLIOTECHNYKH INSTITUTOV. Moscow, Sovetskaia Rossiia, 1957. Both editions may be compared for shifts in ideological orientation.

Diomidova, G.N. BIBLIOGRAFIIA. OBSHCHII KURS. Moscow, Kniga, 1978.

Korshunov, O.P., ed. BIBLIOGRAFIIA. OBSHCHII KURS. Moscow, Kniga, 1981.
rev.: I.E. Barenbaum, SB 2,1982:71-76.

OTRASLEVYE BIBLIOGRAFII. UCHEBNIK DLIA UCHASHCHIKHSIA BIBLIOTECHNYKH TEKHNIKUMOV. 2nd ed. Moscow, Prosveshchenie, 1969.

4.2. Guides

Guides are annotated listings providing access to a wide range of reference sources for a variety of subject areas. In addition to reference works, they may also include major studies in any given field: standard histories, critical editions of classics, legal sources, atlases, etc. They tend to be highly selective in their coverage. They are useful for beginning research and background information in fields secondary to the main focus of the research.

Soviet bibliographers have not produced major guides. But the following might be helpful:

Mez'er, A.V. SLOVARNYI UKAZATEL' PO KNIGOVEDENIIU. Leningrad, Kolos, 1924.

Mez'er, A.V. SLOVARNYI UKAZATEL' PO KNIGOVEDENIIU. Moscow, Gos. sotsial'no-ekonomicheskoe izdatel'stvo, 1931-1934. 3 vols. (A continuation of 1924 ed).

Ienish, op. cit., is useful for information about encyclopedias, dictionaries, statistics, and some directories. Normally, however, a combination of general bibliographic works, guides, and specialized bibliographies will have to be utilized.

The best guide of international scope including the Soviet Union and Eastern Europe is

Sheehy, E.P., ed. GUIDE TO REFERENCE BOOKS. Chicago, Ill., American Library Association, 1976. The 9th edition with subsequent SUPPLEMENTS. Earlier editions were prepared by C.W. Winchell.

We would advise Western scholars to consult Sheehy always as their first source whenever a need for a guide arises in their research.

Standard works published in the West specifically for Russian and Soviet area studies are:

Horecky, P.L., ed. BASIC RUSSIAN PUBLICATIONS. Chicago, University of Chicago Press, 1962.

Horecky, P.L., ed. RUSSIA AND THE SOVIET UNION. A BIBLIOGRAPHIC GUIDE TO WESTERN LANGUAGE PUBLICATIONS. Chicago, University of Chicago Press, 1965.

continued by

Horak, S.M. RUSSIA, THE USSR, AND EASTERN EUROPE. A BIBLIOGRAPHIC GUIDE TO ENGLISH LANGUAGE PUBLICATIONS. 1964-1974. Littleton, Colo., Libraries Unlimited, 1979; and continuation for 1975-1980, published in 1982.

Maichel, K. GUIDE TO RUSSIAN REFERENCE BOOKS. Vol. 1. GENERAL BIBLIOGRAPHIES AND REFERENCE BOOKS. Stanford, Hoover Institution, 1962 (HOOVER INSTITUTION BIBLIOGRAPHICAL SERIES, X). rev.: B.L. Kandel', SB 6,1965:131-139.

Simmons, J.S.G. RUSSIAN BIBLIOGRAPHY, LIBRARY AND ARCHIVES. A SELECTIVE LIST OF BIBLIOGRAPHICAL REFERENCES FOR STUDENTS OF RUSSIAN HISTORY, LITERATURE, POLITICAL, SOCIAL, AND PHILOSOPHICAL THOUGHT, THEOLOGY, AND LINGUISTICS. Oxford, A.C. Hall, 1973. Typewritten supplementary sheets were issued by the author.

de Bonnières, F. GUIDE DE L'ÉTUDIANT EN RUSSE. Paris, Institut d'Études Slaves, 1977 (DOCUMENTS PEDAGOGIQUES DE L'INSTITUT D'ÉTUDES SLAVES, XIV).

Walker, G.P.M.,ed. OFFICIAL PUBLICATIONS OF THE SOVIET UNION AND EASTERN EUROPE, 1945-1980. A SELECTED ANNOTATED BIBLIOGRAPHY. London, Mansell, 1982.
(Although this is not a guide in the strict sense, it has a number of entries of a general character, such as encyclopedias, national bibliographies, statistical sources, and legal documents, which justify its inclusion here.)

Current services:

Zalewski, W. "Reference materials in Russian/Soviet area studies, 1973" in RUSSIAN REVIEW April issues annually since 1975.

Howell, D.L.L. "Russian studies" in THE YEARWORK IN MODERN LANGUAGE STUDIES. Annually.

4.3. Bibliographies of bibliographies

While guides provide answers to almost all basic reference needs, bibliographies of bibliographies attempt to canvas the bibliographic production systematically for a given field. Consequently the beginning of any bibliographic journey is with these.

The majority of bibliographies of bibliographies prepared in the Soviet Union today are based on BIBLIOGRAFIIA SOVETSKOI BIBLIOGRAFII, a series within the national bibliography. It began to appear in 1941 with coverage of 1939, was interrupted during the World War II, and resumed regular publication in 1948 with coverage of 1946. It is issued annually, has introductory surveys by subject, discussing major works for that year, and it cumulates all bibliographies, including those listed within books and articles, registered in any series of the national bibliography.

The Saltykov-Shchedrin Public Library in Leningrad has assumed the primary responsibility for the preparation of scholarly bibliographies of bibliographies. The work was guided by Boris L. Kandel'. His years of efforts and publishing were crowned by a fundamental work which should serve as the beginning of a bibliographic search:

Kandel', B.L. OTECHESTVENNYE UKAZATELI BIBLIOGRAFICHESKIKH POSOBII. Leningrad, [SS], 1983.

The work cumulates earlier surveys published in SS collections: METODICHESKIE MATERIALY V POMOSHCH' BIBLIOTEKAM, RABOTAIUSHCHIM NAD SOSTAVLENIEM BIBLIOGRAFII VTOROI STEPENI (Vypusk 1. Leningrad, 1961) which includes bibliographies of bibliographies for 1842 to 1960. Subsequent issues brought the bibliographic coverage up to 1971. The years 1972 to 1976 were registered in NEKOTORYE ITOGI I PERSPEKTIVY RAZVITIIA BIBLIOGRAFII V SSSR. SBORNIK TRUDOV (Leningrad, 1977) and the years 1978 to 1981 in BIBLIOGRAFIIA BIBLIOGRAFII I EE MESTO V SISTEME NAUCHNOI INFORMATSII. SBORNIK NAUCHNYKH TRUDOV (Leningrad, 1982). The latter work also contains a list of planned bibliographies to be published within the next five years.

For Western readers Kandel' prepared:

"The bibliography of bibliographies in the USSR", UNESCO BULLETIN FOR LIBRARIES 4,1974:217-222.

In addition to the Saltykov-Shchedrin Library various Soviet institutions are producing continuing bibliographic listings of a regional or subject orientation. For information about these see:

Shilstone, M., Zalewski, W. "Current bibliographies in Russian/Soviet area studies," RUSSIAN REVIEW 3, 1978:313-322.

Reshetinskii, I.I. TEKUSHCHIE BIBLIOGRAFICHESKIE IZDANIIA KNIZHNYKH PALAT I IKH ISPOL'ZOVANIE. SPRAVOCHNOE POSOBIE. Moscow, Kniga, 1981.

Andreeva, E.P., et al. PUTEVODITEL' PO IZDANIIAM TEKUSHCHEI OTECHESTVENNOI INFORMATSII: Chast' 1. OBSHCHESTVENNYE NAUKI. Moscow, Kniga, 1981.
Chast' 2 and 3 were published in 1976 and dealt with science and technology.

Major current registrations are:

BIBLIOGRAFIIA SOVETSKOI BIBLIOGRAFII, 1941- was preceded by
Bodnarskii, B.S. in BIBLIOGRAFICHESKIE IZVESTIIA, vols. 1-17, 1913-1929;

and
UKAZATELI BIBLIOGRAFICHESKIKH POSOBII PO OBSHCHESTVENNYM NAUKAM ZA... GOD. Kiev, AN USSR. Biblioteka, 1973-

Retrospective bibliographies of bibliographies are:

Mez'er, A.V., op. cit. (1924):
"Ukazateli knig rukopisnykh", pp. 650-670;
"Ukazateli knig staropechatnykh", pp. 670-673;
"Ukazateli knig grazhdanskoi pechati", pp. 603-631.

Sokurova, M.V. OBSHCHIE BIBLIOGRAFII RUSSKIKH KNIG GRAZHDANSKOI PECHATI, 1708-1955. ANNOTIROVANNYI UKAZATEL'. 2nd ed. Leningrad, 1956.

Works which are international in scope are:

Besterman, T.A. A WORLD BIBLIOGRAPHY OF BIBLIOGRAPHIES AND OF BIBLIOGRAPHICAL CATALOGS, CALENDARS, ABSTRACTS, DIGESTS, INDEXES AND THE LIKE. 4th ed. Lausanne, Societas Bibliographica, 1965-1966. 5 vols.

Staatsbibliothek Preussischer Kulturbesitz. BIBLIOGRAPHISCHE BERICHTE. BIBLIOGRAPHICAL BULLETINS. Frankfurt am Main, Vittorio Klostermann, 1959- annually.

4.4. National bibliography

National bibliographies register publications issued in one country or geographical area. In the Soviet Union, such registration is required by law. In the United States, a legal requirement does not exist (except for the deposit copies of copyrighted materials). The Soviet national bibliography is a comprehensive list of books, pamphlets, dissertation abstracts, music scores, art imprints, cartographic representations, and serials. The content of serials is indexed selectively. This national registration consists of several series which use a standard bibliographic format for every entry and are organized according to 50 standardized subject categories. The national bibliography serves as primary bibliographic source for bibliographic work, and especially for major subject bibliographies, which in most cases are its derivatives. It must be remembered, however, that in various stages of development the national bibliography had various criteria for inclusion, and different bibliographic standards were set. Awareness of these changes is important not only for the proper use of the national bibliography itself, but also for the evaluation of subject bibliographies which emanated from it.

The Russian national bibliography KNIZHNAIA LETOPIS' was established in 1907 (see 2.2.1 above). During the Soviet period, though not earlier than 1926, the bibliography has improved its coverage, both as regards bibliographic standards and subject arrangements, and it has been split into several subseries. While the Vsesoiuznaia Knizhnaia Palata registers in KNIZHNAIA LETOPIS' all monographs which appear on the territory of the Soviet Union in Russian regardless of the original language of publication, republican book chambers register publications issued exclusively on their territory and use the original langauge of publication for their bibliographic entries.

Due to the complexity of the national bibliography in its historic development and contemporary standing, researchers need to be familiar with its basic organization. Information about the national bibliography is available in:

Zdobnov, N.V. op. cit., pp. 216-225, 320-326.

Sokurova, M.V. op. cit., pp. 113-117, 159-167, 179-228 which includes extensive bibliography.

SOROK LET RUSSKOI GOSUDARSTVENNOI BIBLIOGRAFII (1920-1960). SBORNIK STATEI. Moscow, VKP, 1960.

Gracheva, I.B. GOSUDARSTVENNAIA BIBLIOGRAFIIA SSSR. SPRAVOCHNIK. 2nd ed. Moscow, Kniga, 1967. English translation by T.J. Whitby, T. Lorković. INTRODUCTION TO SOVIET NATIONAL BIBLIOGRAPHY. Littleton, Colo., Libraries Unlimited, 1979, with an extensive introduction by Whitby (pp. 15-60) and bibliography (pp. 211-224).

Reviews of many of the series of the national bibliography appeared in the journal SOVETSKAIA BIBLIOGRAFIIA, often in commemoration of an anniversary of the emergence of a subseries.(The index to this journal will help to locate them.)

The following series of the national bibliography represent its status as of 1983. It must be remembered that titles, indexes, and frequency often changed. Information about those changes can be obtained from sources discussing the national bibliography.

Vsesoiuznaia Knizhnaia Palata publishes:

KNIZHNAIA LETOPIS'. OSNOVNOI VYPUSK. 1907- weekly;

KNIZHNAIA LETOPIS'. OSNOVNOI VYPUSK. VSPOMOGATEL'-NYE UKAZATELI. 1907- quarterly;

KNIZHNAIA LETOPIS'. OSNOVNOI VYPUSK. UKAZATEL' SERIINYKH IZDANII. 1933- annual;

KNIZHNAIA LETOPIS'. DOPOLNITEL'NYI VYPUSK. 1961-1980. monthly;

KNIZHNAIA LETOPIS'. DOPOLNITEL'NYI VYPUSK. KNIGI I BROSHIURY. 1981- monthly;

KNIZHNAIA LETOPIS'. DOPOLNITEL'NYI VYPUSK. KNIGI I BROSHIURY. VSPOMOGATEL'NYE UKAZATELI. quarterly;

KNIZHNAIA LETOPIS'. DOPOLNITEL'NYI VYPUSK. UKAZATEL' SERIINYKH IZDANII. annual;

KNIZHNAIA LETOPIS'. DOPOLNITEL'NYI VYPUSK. AVTOREFERATY DISSERTATSII. 1981- monthly;

EZHEGODNIK KNIGI, (1925-1929 as KNIGA V... GODU). 1935. 1941- annual.
In two volumes. Since 1957 the semi-annual publication has changed into two annual volumes:
Vol. 1 covers the Social Sciences and Humanities
Vol. 2 covers Science and Technology.
It cumulates KNIZHNAIA LETOPIS'. OSNOVNOI VYPUSK.
Beginning with 1981 indexes are published separately;

KARTOGRAFICHESKAIA LETOPIS'. 1931- annual;

LETOPIS' IZOIZDANII (since 1976), formerly LETOPIS' PECHATNYKH PROIZVEDENII IZOBRAZITEL'NOGO ISKUSSTVA. 1934- monthly with annual indexes;

NOTNAIA LETOPIS'. 1931- annual.

Lists of periodicals:

LETOPIS' PERIODICHESKIKH IZDANII SSSR. 1933-1954; continued in two series:
Chast' 1. ZHURNALY, TRUDY, BIULLETENI. 1956-
Chast' 2. GAZETY. 1955-
both parts are published every 5 years. The intervals are covered by:

NOVYE, PEREIMENOVANNYE I PREKRASHCHENNYE IZDANIEM ZHURNALY I GAZETY. Annual;

TRUDY, UCHENYE ZAPISKI, SBORNIKI I DRUGIE PRODOLZHAIUSHCHIESIA IZDANIIA. Two issues were published in 1966-1970.

Since 1971 LETOPIS' PERIODICHESKIKH IZDANII has changed its title to:

LETOPIS' PERIODICHESKIKH I PRODOLZHAIUSHCHIKHSIA IZDANII. It has the subseries:

Chast' 1. ZHURNALY. every five years;
Chast' 2. GAZETY. every five years.

SBORNIKI. 1971- annual;

BIULLETENI. 1971- every second year;

NOVYE, PEREIMENOVANNYE I PREKRASHCHENNYE IZDANIEM ZHURNALY I GAZETY, continues as above but not always annually.

Indexes to periodicals:

LETOPIS' ZHURNAL'NYKH STATEI. 1926- weekly; quarterly indexes of personal names and geographic names; annual index of serials indexed;

LETOPIS' GAZETNYKH STATEI. 1936- weekly; quarterly index;

LETOPIS' RETSENZII. 1935- monthly; annual index.

Bibliography of bibliographies:

BIBLIOGRAFIIA SOVETSKOI BIBLIOGRAFII. 1941- annual.

For Republican national bibliographies see Whithby, op. cit., Gracheva, op. cit., SOROK LET...

4.5. Regional bibliographies (Kraevedcheskaia bibliografiia)

Unlike the national and republican bibliographies, which form comprehensive registers of national or republic book and periodical production and give selective indexes of the contents of periodicals, the regional bibliographies attempt to encompass the entire literature devoted to a given region within some specific chronological limits. They are usually prepared by the central public library in the region on the basis of materials received, national and republic bibliographic registration, and an independent bibliographic search. Their periodicity varies from quarterly to irregular, but their titles are somewhat standardized. An example of a title format for a bibliography devoted to a republic is UKRAINSKAIA SSR V IZDANIIAKH RESPUBLIK SOVETSKOGO SOIUZA I STRAN SOTSIALISTICHESKOGO SODRUZHESTVA (Khar'kov, 1967- annual). Other similar bibliographies published within the last five years were devoted to the Armenian, Kazakh, Kirghiz, and Turkmen union republics and, within the RFSFR, the Komi and Udmurt autonomous republics.

Bibliographies devoted to oblasti (regions) have in most cases a descriptive title, e.g., LITERATURA O...(VOLOGODSKOI OBLASTI) ZA...GOD (Vologda, 1961- annual). The following Russian and Ukrainian oblast' and krai are covered under similar formats: Arkhangel'skaia, Astrakhanskaia, Brianskaia, Cheliabinskaia, Chernigovskaia, Chitinskaia, Irkutskaia, Ivanovskaia, Kaliningradskaia, Kaluzhskaia, Kemerovskaia, Khmel'nitskaia, Kievskaia, Kirovo-gradskaia, Krasnoiarskaia, Kuibyshevskaia, L'vovskaia, Moskovskaia, Murmanskaia, Novgorodskaia, Omskaia, Orlovskaia, Penzenskaia, Rostovskaia, Sakhalinskaia, Saratovskaia, Sverdlovskaia, Tarnopol'skaia, Tul'skaia, Ul'ianovskaia, Volgogradskaia, Voronezhskaia, and West Siberia.

Special bibliographies are devoted to Kiev--GOROD KIEV I KIEVSKAIA OBLAST' (Kiev, 1974 for 1971-72, 116 pp.)--and Moscow--NOVAIA LITERATURA O MOSKVE (Moscow, 1960- monthly), a systematic list of books and articles relating to society and culture in contemporary and historical Moscow.

For this broad field, consult the following sources:

Mamontov, A.V. KRAEVEDCHESKAIA BIBLIOGRAFIIA V ROSSII V DOREVOLIUTSIONNYI PERIOD. UCHEBNOE POSOBIE DLIA STUDENTOV BIBLIOTECHNYKH FAKUL'TETOV. Leningrad, 1974.

Mamontov, A.V., Shcherba. N.N. KRAEVEDCHESKAIA BIBLIOGRAFIIA. UCHEBNIK DLIA BIBLIOGRAFICHESKIKH FAKUL'TETOV INST. KUL'TURY I PED. VUZOV. Moscow, Kniga, 1978.

Briskman, M.A. OSNOVNYE ISTOCHNIKI BIBLIOGRAFICHESKIKH RAZYSKANII PO KRAEVEDENIIU. UCHEBNOE POSOBIE DLIA STUDENTOV BIBLIOTECHNYKH FAKUL'TETOV.Vyp.l. Leningrad, 1974.

Ozerova, G.A. BIBLIOGRAFIIA KRAEVEDCHESKOI BIBLIOGRAFII RSFSR V DEVIATOI I DESIATOI PIATILETKAKH. VOPROSY ISTORII I METODIKI UNIVERSAL'NOI I OTRASLEVOI BIBLIOGRAFII BIBLIOGRAFII. SBORNIK NAUCHNYKH TRUDOV. Leningrad, [SS], 1980:5-19.

KRAEVEDCHESKAIA BIBLIOGRAFIIA (SOSTOIANIE I PERSPEKTIVY RAZVITIIA) SBORNIK NAUCHNYKH TRUDOV. Novosibirsk. AN SSSR Sibirskoe otdelenie, 1976 and especially here: A.V. Mamontov, "Sistema kraevedcheskikh bibliograficheskikh posobii" (pp. 5-29).

Titova, Z.D. OBSHCHIE I OTRASLEVYE BIBLIOGRAFII KAK ISTOCHNIK KRAEVEDCHESKOI BIBLIOGRAFII RSFSR. Leningrad,[SS],1964 and continuation in

BIBLIOGRAFIIA KRAEVEDCHESKOI BIBLIOGRAFII RSFSR: ANNOTIROVANNYI UKAZATEL':
Chast' 1. Z.D. Titova. OBSHCHIE I OTRASLEVYE UKAZATELI KAK ISTOCHNIK KRAEVEDCHESKOI BIBLIOGRAFII RSFSR. 1961-1975 gg. Leningrad, [SS], 1979, (same title for individual regions published in separate volumes since 1963);
Chast' 2. G.A. Ozerova, Z.D. Titova. BIBLIOGRAFIIA GEOGRAFICHESKIKH I EKONOMICHESKIKH RAIONOV, KRAEV, OBLASTEI I AVTONOMNYKH RESPUBLIK RSFSR. Leningrad, [SS], 1978.

For additional titles of bibliographies of bibliographies in this field see B.L. Kandel' OTECHESTVENNYE UKAZATEL... pp. 64-73. The majority of souces that Kandel' lists were published in a limited number of copies by the Saltykov-Shchedrin Library in Leningrad and were not available commercially.

Sections entitled "Kraevedcheskaia bibliografiia" in the BIBLIOGRAFIIA SOVETSKOI BIBLIOGRAFII and "Otraslevye bibliograficheskie ukazateli" in the LETOPIS' PERIODICHESKIKH I PRODOLZHAIUSHCHIKHSIA IZDANII. BIULLETENI are helpful in identifying regional bibliographies.

Users of the regional bibliographies are reminded that often those bibliographies are recommendatory rather than scholarly and may not be satisfactory for research purposes.

4.6. Format bibliographies

4.6.1. Books

In our earlier discussion of catalogs we indicated sources which are most suitable for identifying publications up to the end of the eighteen century. To this list we may add two important bibliographies which, however, retain primarily historic value. They offer a different subject approach than the Soviet produced catalogs. They include pre-Petrine imprints, and Smirdin's catalog extends coverage into the nineteenth century. These bibliographies are:

Sopikov, V.S. OPYT ROSSIISKOI BIBLIOGRAFII, 2nd edition by V.N. Rogozhin. St. Petersburg, A.S. Suvorin, 1904-1908. 5 vols.

Smirdin, A.F. (Firm). ROSPIS' ROSSIISKIM KNIGAM DLIA CHTENIIA, IZ BIBLIOTEKI ALEKSANDRA SMIRDINA. V.G. Anastasevich, ed. St. Petersburg, A. Smirdin, 1828-1856. 5 vols.

A comprehensive bibliography of the nineteenth century Russian imprints is being prepared and it probably will be published toward the end of this century. Until then, several other sources must be used. We have indicated so far the national bibliography, which is difficult to use, and the catalogs of the Helsinki and Leningrad University Libraries. However, the best bibliographies for the first three quarters of the nineteenth century are the commercial catalog-bibliographies. The best bibliographers, such as V.I. Mezhov and P.A. Efremov, were employed by book dealers to prepare catalogs of their bookstore holdings. The compilers, however, often exceeded stock on hand and listed other books in print, thus offering an extensive bibliography of works published. Subject approach, indexes, even indication of book reviews add to the value of these sources.

V.O. Osipov offers overview of the book trade catalogs in his

KNIGOTORGOVAIA BIBLIOGRAFIIA. Moscow, Kniga, 1976, 2nd edition: Moscow, Kniga, 1984, and in some works edited by him:

RUSSKAIA KNIGOTORGOVAIA BIBLIOGRAFIIA DO NACHALA XX v. Moscow, Kniga, 1983;

KNIGOTORGOVYE KATALOGI PERVOI POLOVINY XIX VEKA. UKAZATEL'. UCHEBNOE POSOBIE. Moscow, Kniga, 1976;

KNIGOTORGOVYE KATALOGI 50-60 GG. XIX VEKA. UKAZATEL'. UCHEBNOE POSOBIE. Moscow, Kniga, 1980;

KNIGOTORGOVYE KATALOGI 60-70-KH GG. XIX VEKA. UKAZATEL'. UCHEBNOE POSOBIE. Moscow,Kniga, 1980.

The most important trade catalogs are:

Bazunov, A.F. (Firm). SISTEMATICHESKII KATALOG RUSSKIM KNIGAM PRODAIUSHCHIMSIA V KNIZHNOM MAGAZINIE ALEKSANDRA FEDOROVICHA BAZUNOVA, S UKAZANIEM 20,000 KRITICHESKIKH STATEI, RETSENZII I BIBLIOGRAFICHESKIKH ZAMETOK...St.Petersburg, A.F. Bazunov, 1869-1880. 10 Supplements. Supplements 7-8 were produced by the Ia. A. Isakov Firm.

Glazunov, I.I. (Firm). SISTEMATICHESKAIA ROSPIS' KNIGAM... St.Petersburg, I.I. Glazunov, 1867-1889. 5 Supplements.

These catalogs extend bibliographic coverage to imprints published up to 1887. Another dimension is added by:

SVODNYI KATALOG RUSSKOI NELEGAL'NOI I ZAPRESHCHENNOI PECHATI XIX VEKA. KNIGI I PERIODICHESKIE IZDANIIA. I.V. Morozova, ed. 2nd ed. Moscow, 1981-1982. 2 vols.;
and the same title for LISTOVKI. Moscow, 1977. 3 parts.

A useful but selective bibliography is:

Rubakin, N.A. SREDI KNIG. 2nd ed. Moscow, Nauka, 1911-1916. 3 vols. (Has extensive historiographic introductions.)

The overall coverage of the nineteenth century Russian imprints is poor. Some fields, however, have excellent subject bibliographies (see Part II). There are also bibliographies of society or publishing house publications, indexes to periodicals, and catalogs to private collections, all of which extend the bibliographic search, but without assurance of comprehensiveness. The period 1900-1917 suffers particularly severe limitations. Beginning with 1907, the national bibliography KNIZHNAIA LETOPIS' has provided somewhat more reliable bibliographic data. It carries into the Soviet era and it is the only general bibliography covering that period.

Книжная Лѣтопись

Главнаго Управленія по дѣламъ печати.

№ 1. **1907 г.** **14 іюля.**

Библіографическимъ отдѣломъ Главнаго Управленія по дѣламъ печати, при которомъ сосредоточено полученіе обязательныхъ экземпляровъ всѣхъ вновь выходящихъ въ Россіи книгъ и снабженіе ими государственныхъ книгохранилищъ, 1-го сего іюля введена новая система регистраціи книгъ. Результаты этой регистраціи будутъ опубликовываться еженедѣльно въ „Книжной Лѣтописи Главнаго Управленія по дѣламъ печати". Давая такимъ путемъ возможность всѣмъ интересующимся книжнымъ дѣломъ своевременно получать не только полные списки всѣхъ вновь выходящихъ книгъ, но и подробныя библіографическія ихъ описанія, удовлетворяющія какъ научнымъ, такъ и практическимъ требованіямъ, „Книжная Лѣтопись Главнаго Управленія по дѣламъ печати" будетъ выходить по слѣдующей программѣ:

I. Еженедѣльно.

1. а) Перечень въ алфавитномъ порядкѣ книгъ, напечатанныхъ въ Россіи какъ на русскомъ такъ и на другихъ языкахъ;
   б) Предметный указатель, представляющій собою сводъ всего напечатаннаго за недѣлю.
2. а) Перечень выдающихся статей нѣкоторыхъ русскихъ журналовъ и газетъ;
   б) Перечень отзывовъ и рецензій о вновь вышедшихъ книгахъ;
   в) Разныя извѣстія, касающіяся книгопечатанія и книжной торговли;
   г) Объявленія.

4.6.2. Serials

Serials are publications issued in parts over an indefinite period of time. They include continuing series of monographic publications, regular and irregular scholarly and professional journals, magazines of interest to particular groups or to the general public, and newspapers. Serials are bibliographically complex since they often merge with each other, change title, format, arrangement, periodicity, etc. Consequently, an understanding of the publishing history of serials and of their formats is very useful for bibliographic work. For example, a diversity of subjects and treatments packed into one issue was characteristic for nineteenth-century Russian journals, the so-called "thick journals." An academic serial carried both articles and monographs; Soviet serialized collections of papers (SBORNIK TRUDOV, TRUDY, or UCHENYE ZAPISKI) are issued with great irregularity, frequent title changes, change in physical format, etc.

Russian and Soviet serials have been listed comprehensively in bibliographies, but indexes to serials are not comprehensive. Masanov's work (below) permits the identification of existing indexes. Parts of the national bibliography (see above), index journals, newspapers, and reviews. Of course, subject bibliographies provide the best information on the content of serials. Users of subject bibliographies must be aware, however, whether the compiler conducted an independent bibliographic search of periodical literature, as in the case of most pre-revolutionary bibliographers, or relied exclusively on national bibliographies, as quite often may be the case with Soviet bibliographers.

4.6.2.1. Histories of periodicals

Mez'er, A.V., op. cit. (1924), pp. 231-323 (includes bibliographies on history, lists, and indexes).

Zapadov, V.A. ISTORIIA RUSSKOI ZHURNALISTIKI XVIII-XIX v. Moscow, Vysshaia shkola, 1973. (Including bibliography).

IZ ISTORII RUSSKOI ZHURNALISTIKI KONTSA XIX-NACHALA XX v. B.I. Esin, ed. Moscow, Universitet, 1973.

Esin, B.I. RUSSKAIA DOREVOLIUTSIONNAIA GAZETA. 1702-1917. Moscow, 1971.

Rubakin, N.A. SREDI KNIG. Moscow, Nauka, 1971, Vol. 1, pp. 204-254; 296-307. (Including bibliography).

Stan'ko, A.I. RUSSKIE GAZETY PERVOI POLOVINY XIX V. Rostov, Universitet, 1969.

Kuznetsov, I.V. GAZETNYI MIR SOVETSKOGO SOIUZA. 1917-1970 GG. Moscow, Universitet, 1972-1976.
Vol. 1. TSENTRAL'NYE GAZETY.
Vol. 2. RESPUBLIKANSKIE, KRAEVYE, OBLASTNYE I OKRUZHNYE GAZETY.

4.6.2.2. Lists of periodicals

4.6.2.2.1. Bibliography of bibliographies

Zdobnov, N.V., op. cit., pp. 349-360;

Andreeva, N.F., RUSSKAIA PERIODICHESKAIA PECHAT'. OBSHCHIE I OTRASLEVYE BIBLIOGRAFICHESKIE UKAZATELI, 1703-1975. 2nd ed. Moscow, Kniga, 1977.

4.6.2.2.2. Lists

Lisovskii, N.M. RUSSKAIA PERIODICHESKAIA PECHAT'. 1703-1900 GG. BIBLIOGRAFIIA I GRAFICHESKIE TABLITSY. Petrograd, 1915.

Sreznevskii, V.I. SPISOK RUSSKIKH POVREMENNYKH IZDANII S 1703 PO 1899 GOD S SVEDENEM O EKZEMPLIARAKH, PRINADLEZHASHCHIKH BIBLIOTEKE IMP. AKADEMII NAUK. St.Petersburg, 1901. (Retains value for about 250 titles not listed in Lisovskii).

SVODNYI KATALOG RUSSKOI KNIGI GRAZHDANSKOI PECHATI XVIII V. T.IV. PERIODICHESKIE I PRODOLZHAIUSHCHIESIA IZDANIIA... and Supplement, 1975.

BIBLIOGRAFIIA PERIODICHESKIKH IZDANII ROSSII: 1901-1916. L.M. Beliaeva, et al., eds. Leningrad, 1958-1961. 4 vols.

PERIODICHESKAIA PECHAT' SSSR, 1917-1949. BIBLIOGRAFICHESKII UKAZATEL'. Moscow, VKP, 1955-1963. 10 vols. (Vol. 10 is an index).

GAZETY SSSR, 1917-1960:
Tom 1. Moscow, Kniga, 1970.
Tom 2. Chast' 1. Moscow, Kniga, 1976.
Tom 3. Moscow, Kniga, 1978 (for Republics).
Continued by LETOPIS' PERIODICHESKIKH IZDANII.
(See national bibliography.)

Descriptive but selective lists and histories of periodicals are:

Dement'ev, A.B. RUSSKAIA PERIODICHESKAIA PECHAT'. 1702-1894. SPRAVOCHNIK. Moscow, Gospolitizdat, 1959.

Cherepakov, M.S. RUSSKAIA PERIODICHESKAIA PECHAT' 1895-OKT. 1917. Moscow, Gospolitizdat, 1957.

See also library catalogs.

4.6.2.3. Indexes to periodicals

4.6.2.3.1. Bibliographies of indexes

Mez'er, A.V.: see histories of periodicals.

Masanov, Iu.F. UKAZATELI SODERZHANIIA RUSSKIKH ZHURNALOV I PRODOLZHAIUSHCHIKHSIA IZDANII, 1755-1970 GG. Moscow, Kniga, 1975.

Suvorova, A.V. "Ukazateli soderzhaniia mestnykh periodicheskikh izdanii (1847-1917 gg)", BIBLIOGRAFIIA V POMOSHCH' NAUKE. Leningrad,1977: 92-106.(Leningradskii Gos. inst. kul'tury. TRUDY XXXIV.)

4.6.2.3.2. Indexes

Neustroev, A.N. UKAZATEL' K RUSSKIM POVREMENNYM IZDANIIAM I SBORNIKAM ZA 1703-1802 I K "ISTORICHESKOMU ROZYSKANIIU" O NIKH. St.Petersburg,1898. For additions see: L. Maikov, "Neskol'ko dannykh dlia istorii russkoi zhurnalistiki", OCHERKI IZ ISTORII RUSSKOI LITERATURY XVII-XVIII V. St. Petersburg, 1889: 69-424.

Popov, V.A. SISTEMATICHESKII UKAZATEL' STATEI, POMESHCHENNYKH V. ... PERIODICHESKIKH IZD. S 1830 PO 1884 g. St. Petersburg, 1885.

Ul'ianov, N.A. UKAZATEL' ZHURNAL'NOI LITERATURY. 1896-1910. Moscow, 1811-1913. 2 vyp.

For current indexes see national bibliography:

LETOPIS' ZHURNAL'NYH STATEI;
LETOPIS' GAZETNYKH STATEI;
LETOPIS' RETSENZII.

4.6.2.4. Directories of periodicals

Birkos, A.S., Tambs, L.A. ACADEMIC WRITER'S GUIDE TO PERIODICALS. II. EAST EUROPEAN AND SLAVIC STUDIES. Kent, Ohio, 1973.

4.6.3. Dissertations (typescripts)

Copies of Soviet dissertations are kept by the sponsoring institutions and are deposited in the Lenin Public Library in Moscow. This Library produces monthly lists:

KATALOG KANDIDATSKIKH I DOKTORSKIKH DISSERTATSII, POSTUPIVSHIKH V BIBLIOTEKU SSSR IM. V.I. LENINA I V GOSUDARSTVENNUIU TSENTRAL'NUIU NAUCHNUIU MEDITSINSKUIU BIBLIOTEKU. Moscow, 1956-

Additionally, dissertation abstracts have been registered in various series of the national bibliography at various times (see A.L. Shapiro, BIBLIOGRAFIIA ISTORII SSSR, Moscow, 1968: 49-51). In 1981 the KNIZHNAIA LETOPIS'. DOPOLNITEL'NYI

VYPUSK split in two parts, of which the AVTOREFERATY DISSERTATSII registers abstracts exclusively. All of these sources are difficult to use since they are not cumulated. There are bibliographies of dissertations defended in a given subject listed in subject bibliographies, e.g., XVIII VEK, Vyp.3, Leningrad, 1958. Some institutions have retrospective bibliographies, e.g., DISSERTATSII, ZASHCHISHCHENNYE V TARTUSKOM UNIVERSITETE, 1802-1919, BIBLIOGRAFICHESKII UKAZATEL'. Tartu, 1973. It must be noted that Western scholars and libraries cannot obtain Soviet dissertations through commercial or exchange channels; the abstracts (avtoreferaty), however, can be filmed and exported.

Typescripts in the social sciences and humanities are deposited in the INION's library and listed annually in

KATALOG DEPONIROVANNYKH RUKOPISEI: OBSHCHESTVENNYE NAUKI, 1976-. Moscow, 1977-

VINITI fulfills similar function in the sciences:

DEPONIROVANNYE RUKOPISI: ESTESTVENNYE I TOCHNYE NAUKI, TEKHNIKA. Moscow, 1963-

For additional information about Soviet and Western dissertations see J.S.G. Simmons, op. cit., pp. 25-26.

The best source for American dissertations is:

Dossick, J.J. DOCTORAL RESEARCH ON RUSSIA AND THE SOVIET UNION. New York, New York University Press, 1960, continued for 1960-1975 (New York, Garland, 1976) and updated annually in the SLAVIC REVIEW.

see also

COMPREHENSIVE DISSERTATION INDEX 1861-1972. Ann Arbor, Xerox University Microfilms, 1973.

Continuation in DISSERTATION ABSTRACTS and similar registrations for other countries. For those consult Sheehy, op. cit.

Terry, G.M. "A guide to bibliographies of theses and dissertations in the field of Slavonic and East European studies." ABSSES 4,1976:I-XXVIII.

4.6.4. Manuscripts

Catalogs to libraries and archives are the most important bibliographic sources for manuscripts and manuscript books. Consequently scholars are referred chapters on archives, library catalogs, and dissertations listed in both the gereral and the subject parts of our work.

A journal of scholarly and bibliographic importance is

ARKHEOGRAFICHESKII EZHEGODNIK, 1957-

4.7. Publisher's bibliographies

The importance of familiarity with the publishing in Russia for bibliographic work has been stressed already. For almost every discipline, publishing houses of importance may be identified. Some houses maintain obvious scholarly standards, e.g., the Academy of Sciences, or subject profiles, which typifies the majority of publishing houses in the Soviet Union, while still others are diversified. Institutions often issue catalogs of their publications. These, although not exhaustive from the bibliographic point of view, can offer invaluable assistance in locating major works on a given subject and facilitate an extended follow-up bibliographic search. Such catalogs can be identified either through bibliographies of bibliographies or through a search under the publisher's name in catalogs of major libraries. Part II lists some subject - oriented publishers' catalogs.

The Acadamy of Sciences provides a good example of a multi-subject catalog-bibliography:

KATALOG IZDANII IMP. AKADEMII NAUK. St.Petersburg, Akademiia Nauk, 1912-1916. 3 vols. Supplement, 1942.

SISTEMATICHESKII UKAZATEL' IZDANII AN SSSR, VYSHEDSHIKH V SVET S 1 IANVARIA 1917 G. PO 1 SENTIABRIA 1925 G. Leningrad, AN SSSR, 1925.

KATALOG KNIG IZDATEL'STVA AKADEMII NAUK SSSR, 1945-1962. Moscow, Nauka, 1965; continues now as KATALOG KNIG IZDATEL'STVA NAUKA, 1963-1967. Moscow, Nauka, 1971-

and the most important of such catalogs, which is quite often overlooked as a bibliographic tool:

BIBLIOGRAFICHESKII UKAZATEL' IZDANII, OPUBLIKOVANNYKH ADADEMIEI NAUK SSSR. Leningrad, 1930-, published since 1956 as BIBLIOGRAFIIA IZDANII AKADEMII NAUK SSSR. (Annual). This serves not only as a bibliography of books but also as an index to all journals, collected works, papers, conferences, etc. published by the Academy of Sciences and all its branches. At the same time it provides the best available overview of ongoing Soviet research.

Helpful can also be:

KATALOG IMEIUSHCHIKHSIA V PRODAZHE IZDANII AKADEMII NAUK. 1769-1935. Moscow-Leningrad, AN SSSR, 1936.

There are also retrospective and current bibliographies of academic institutions. For these see

Shapiro, op. cit., pp. 276-282.

An example of such a bibliography is

PECHATNYE TRUDY I DISSERTATSII MOSKOVSKOGO UNIVERSITETA. BIBLIOGRAFICHESKII UKAZATEL'... GOD.

4.8. Western language materials

4.8.1. Catalogs

BIBLIOTHÈQUE IMPÉRIALE DE ST.-PÉTERSBOURG. CATALOGUE DE LA SECTION DES RUSSICA OU ÉCRITS SUR LA RUSSIE EN LANGUAGES ÉTRANGÈRES. St. Petersburg, 1873. 2 vols.

and a subject-oriented catalog:

Gol'dberg, A.L., Iakovleva, I.G. DOREVOLIUTSIONNYE IZDANIIA PO ISTORII SSSR V INOSTRANNOM FONDE GOSUDARSTVENNOI PUBLICHNOI BIBLIOTEKI IM. M.E. SALTYKOVA-SHCHEDRINA. SISTEMATICHESKII UKAZATEL' Vyp. I, Leningrad, 1982-

Both sources can be used in addition to R.J. Kerner (below).

4.8.2. Current bibliographies

Western Europe:

EUROPEAN BIBLIOGRAPHY OF SOVIET, EAST EUROPEAN, AND SLAVONIC STUDIES, 1975- Birmingham, 1978- . It was preceded by registration in the journals:

CAHIERS DU MONDE RUSSE ET SOVIETIQUE;
SOVIET, EAST EUROPEAN AND SLAVONIC STUDIES.

For non participating countries see:
RICHERCHE SLAVISTICHE (Italy);
SCANDO-SLAVICA (Scandinavian countries except Finland).

East Germany:

Pohrt, H. BIBLIOGRAPHIE SLAVISCHER PUBLIKAZIONEN AUS DER DEUTSCHEN DEMOKRATISCHEN REPUBLIK, 1946-1967. Berlin, Akademischer Verlag, 1968- (latest:1978-1981. 1983).

Canada:

Stevens, M. "Canadian publications on the Soviet Union and Easten Europe for...", CANADIAN SLAVO-

NIC PAPERS, 1978-

United States:

AMERICAN BIBLIOGRAPHY OF SLAVIC AND EAST EUROPEAN STUDIES, 1956-

4.8.3. Retrospective bibliographies

Kerner, R.J. SLAVIC EUROPE. A SELECTED BIBLIOGRAPHY IN THE WESTERN EUROPEAN LANGUAGES. Cambridge, Harvard University Press, 1918.

Grierson, P. BOOKS ON SOVIET RUSSIA 1917-1942. A BIBLIOGRAPHY AND A GUIDE TO READING. London, Methuen, 1943.

Schultheiss, Th., ed. RUSSIAN STUDIES 1941-1958. A CUMULATION OF THE ANNUAL BIBLIOGRAPHIES FROM THE RUSSIAN REVIEW. Ann Arbor, The Pierian Press, 1972.

Jones, D.L. BOOKS IN ENGLISH ON THE SOVIET UNION 1917-73. A BIBLIOGRAPHY. New York, Garland, 1975.

4.8.4. Serials

For serials in Western languages see:

J.W. Hoskins, op. cit.

F. de Bonnières, GUIDE...

Part I.4.8.2 (current bibliographies).

4.9. Émigré publications

4.9.1. Monographs

Postnikov, S.P. RUSSKAIA ZARUBEZHNAIA KNIGA. Prague, "Plamia," 1924. 2 vols. (for 1918-1924).

MATERIALY DLIA BIBLIOGRAFII RUSSKIKH NAUCHNYKH TRUDOV ZA RUBEZHOM 1920-1940. Belgrade, Russkii nauchnyi institut, 1931-1940. 2 vols.

Schatoff, M.V. "Bibliograficheskii ukazatel' russkoi pechati za rubezhom..." MOSTY 3, 1959- (FOR 1957-1958) continued by his BIBLIOGRAPHICAL INDEX OF RUSSIAN PUBLICATIONS OUTSIDE OF THE USSR. New York, 1964-1967. (for 1961-1964).

Bibliography in MOSTY has also been published separately.

Commercial catalogs:

RUSSKIE KNIGI by Niemanis (Munich);
Les Editeurs Reunis (Paris);
Possev (Frankfurt am Main);
Ardis (Ann Arbor, Mich.).

See also Part II.3.8.

Woll, J. SOVIET DISSIDENT LITERATURE. A CRITICAL GUIDE. Boston, G.K. Hall, 1983.

Woll, J. SOVIET UNOFFICIAL LITERATURE. AN ANNOTATED BIBLIOGRAPHY OF WORKS PUBLISHED IN THE WEST. Durham, N.C., Duke University Center for International Studies, 1978.

4.9.2. Serials

4.9.2.1. Lists

Schatoff, M. HALF A CENTURY OF RUSSIAN SERIALS, 1917-1968. CUMULATIVE INDEX OF SERIALS PUBLISHED OUTSIDE THE USSR. New York, Russian Book Chamber Abroad, 1969-1972. 4 vols.

UKAZATEL' PERIODICHESKIKH IZDANII EMIGRATSII IZ ROSSII I SSSR, 1919-1952. München, 1953. (Institut po izucheniiu istorii i kul'tury SSSR. ISSLEDOVANIIA I MATERIALY, 6).

See also Part I. 3.1.3.5.

4.9.2.2. Indexes

Khotin, L., ed. ABSTRACTS OF SOVIET AND EAST EUROPEAN PERIODICAL LITERATURE. Pacific Grove, CA., 1981-

See also AMERICAN BIBLIOGRAPHY OF SLAVIC AND EAST EURPOPEAN STUDIES.

Indexes to individual periodicals:

SOVREMENNYE ZAPISKI (1938);
GRANI (1977);
NOVYI ZHURNAL (1970).

5. Non-bibliographic reference sources (Spravochniki)

5.1. Bibliography

The pre-revolutionary period is well covered by an outstanding bibliography:

Zaionchkovskii, P.A. SPRAVOCHNIKI PO ISTORII DOREVOLIUTSIONNOI ROSSII. Moscow, Kniga, 1971. 2nd ed., significantly revised, 1978.

During the post-revolutionary period production of general information sources declined sharply. Bibliographies of such sources are not very satisfactory, and are scattered through various guides.

A recently published source is:

E.V. Gol'tseva, et al., OT RUKOPISI - K KNIGE, SPRAVOCHNYE IZDANIIA. SPETSIFICHESKIE OSOBENNOSTI I TREBOVANIIA. Moscow, Kniga, 1982.

5.2. Encyclopedias

5.2.1. General

In addition to Gol'tseva, op. cit., see:

Seydoux, M. "Les encyclopédies générales russes: essai bibliographique", CAHIERS DU MONDE RUSSE ET SOVIETIQUE VI, 1965: 245-263;

Kaufman, I.M. RUSSKIE ENTSIKLOPEDII. Vyp. 1 OBSHCHIE ENTSIKLOPEDII. Moscow, 1960.

Shmushkis, I.E. SOVETSKIE ENTSIKLOPEDII. OCHERKI ISTORII, VOPROSY METODIKI. Moscow, Sovetskaia Entsiklopediia, 1975.

Major general encyclopedias are:

ENTSIKLOPEDICHESKII SLOVAR'. I.E. Andreevskii, ed. St.Petersburg, F.A. Brokgauz, I.A. Efron, 1890-1907. 41 Vols.

NOVYI ENTSIKLOPEDICHESKII SLOVAR'. K.K. Arsen'ev, ed. St.Petersburg, 1911-1916. 29 Vols. A-Otto.

BOL'SHAIA ENTSIKLOPEDIIA. S.N. Iuzhakov, P.N. Miliukov, eds. St. Petersburg, Meier, Knigoizdatel'skoe tovarishchestvo Prosveshchenie, 1900-1909. 22 Vols.

ENTSIKLOPEDICHESKII SLOVAR' T-VA "BR. A. I I. GRANAT I KO". M.M. Kovalevskii, S.A. Muromtsev, K.A. Timiriazev, eds. 7th ed. Moscow, Granat, [1910]-1948. Vols. 1-55, 57-58, dop. 1.

BOL'SHAIA SOVETSKAIA ENTSIKLOPEDIIA. O.Iu. Shmidt, ed. Moscow, Sovetskaia Entsiklopediia, 1926-1948. 65 vols.
Supplement: SOIUZ SOVETSKIKH SOTSIALISTICHESKIKH RESPUBLIK. 1947.

BOL'SHAIA SOVETSKAIA ENTSIKLOPEDIIA. S.I. Vavilov, B.A. Vvedenskii, eds. Moscow, Sovetskaia Entsiklopediia, 1950-1960. 50 vols.
Vol. 50: SOIUZ SOVETSKIKH SOTSIALISTICHESKIKH RESPUBLIK. 1957. Also published separately as SSSR. 1957.
ALFAVITNYI UKAZATEL' KO VTOROMU IZDANIIU. 2 vols. [1960].
EZHEGODNIK, 1957-

BOL'SHAIA SOVETSKAIA ENTSIKLOPEDIIA. A.M. Prokhorov, ed. Moscow, Sovetskaia Entsiklopediia, 1969-1978. 30 vols.
ALFAVITNYI IMMENNOI UKAZATEL'. 1981.
Supplement: SSSR. ENTSIKLOPEDICHESKII SPRAVOCHNIK. 1982. This volume is updated periodically.

The three editions of BOL'SHAIA SOVETSKAIA ENTSIKLOPEDIIA continue rather than replace each other. Each reflects the political climate of its time. Bibliographies accompanying articles do not repeat earlier listings but update them. Each set has a long section on Russia/USSR. The encyclopedia is updated annually by EZHEGODNIK, 1956- which technically ties up with the second edition.

A handy one volume encyclopedia is

SOVETSKII ENTSIKLOPEDICHESKII SLOVAR'. A.M. Prokhorov, ed. Moscow, Sovetskaia Entsiklopediia, 1st ed., 1979; 2nd ed., 1982; 3rd ed., 1984.

The translation of the 3rd edition of the BOL'SHAIA SOVETSKAIA ENTSIKLOPEDIIA is available in English, namely:

GREAT SOVIET ENCYCLOPEDIA. A TRANSLATION OF THE THIRD EDITION. New York, Macmillan, 1973-

An earlier translation of vol. 50 of the 2nd edition of BOL'SHAIA SOVETSKAIA ENTSIKLOPEDIIA with some addenda by the editor is

INFORMATION USSR. AN AUTHORITATIVE ENCYCLOPEDIA ABOUT THE UNION OF SOVIET SOCIALIST REPUBLICS. R. Maxwell, ed. Oxford, Pergamon, 1962.

Addressed to the reading audience at large is

THE CAMBRIDGE ENCYCLOPEDIA OF RUSSIA AND THE SOVIET UNION. A. Brown, et al., eds. Cambridge, Eng., Cambridge University Press, 1982.

For older encyclopedias consult the guides by Kaufman and Shmushkis, both cited above.

5.2.2. Subject encyclopedias

Bibliography:

Kaufman, I.M. TERMINOLOGICHESKIE SLOVARI. BIBLIOGRAFIIA. Moscow, Sovetskaia Rossiia, 1961.

Selected encyclopedias:

(Publisher is Moscow, Sovetskaia entsiklopediia, unless otherwise indicated).

BALET. ENTSIKLOPEDIIA. 1981.

DIPLOMATICHESKII SLOVAR'. 1948-1959. 2 vols.; Moscow, Politizdat, 1971-1973. 3 vols. Moscow, Nauka, 1983-

EKONOMICHESKAIA ENTSIKLOPEDIIA. POLITICHESKAIA EKONOMIIA. 1972. 4 vols.

EKONOMICHESKAIA ENTSIKLOPEDIIA. PROMYSHLENNOST' I STROITEL'STVO. There were the following editions: 1932-1936;
1938-1940;
1949-1956;
1962-1965. 3 vols.

ENTSIKLOPEDICHESKII MUZYKAL'NYI SLOVAR'. 1959. 2nd ed. 1966.

ENTSIKLOPEDICHESKII SLOVAR' GEOGRAFICHESKIKH NAZVANII. 1973.

ENTSIKLOPEDIIA GOSUDARSTVA I PRAVA. Moscow, Izd-vo Komunisticheskoi Akademii, 1925-1927; 2nd ed., 1929-1930. 3 vols.

FILOSOFSKAIA ENTSIKLOPEDIIA. 1960-1970. 5 vols.

FILOSOFSKII ENTSIKLOPEDICHESKII SLOVAR'. 1983.

FILOSOFSKII SLOVAR'. Moscow, Politizdat, 1963; 2nd ed., 1968; 3rd ed., 1972; 4th ed., 1980.

FILOSOFSKII SLOVAR'. Moscow, Progress, 1983.

FINANSOVAIA ENTSIKLOPEDIIA. Moscow, Gos.izdatel'-stvo, 1927.

FINANSOVO-KREDITNYI SLOVAR'. Moscow, Gosfinizdat, 1961-1964. 2 vols.

GRAZHDANSKAIA VOINA I VOENNAIA INTERVENTSIIA V SSSR. ENTSIKLOPEDIIA. 1983.

IURIDICHESKII SLOVAR'. Moscow, Gosiurizdat, 1953. 2nd ed. 1956. 2 vols.

KINO-SLOVAR'. 1966-1970. 2 vols.

KNIGOVEDENIE. ENTSIKLOPEDICHESKII SLOVAR'. 1982.

KRATKAIA GEOGRAFICHESKAIA ENTSIKLOPEDIIA. 1960-1966. 5 vols.

KRATKAIA LITERATURNAIA ENTSIKLOPEDIIA. 1962-1978. 9 vols.

KURORTY. ENTSIKLOPEDICHESKII SLOVAR'. 1982.

LERMONTOVSKAIA ENTSIKLOPEDIIA. 1981.

LITERATURNAIA ENTSIKLOPEDIIA. SLOVAR' LITERATURNYKH TERMINOV. Moscow-Leningrad, Frenkel', 1925. 2 vols.

LITERATURNAIA ENTSIKLOPEDIIA. Moscow, Izd-vo Kommunisticheskoi Akademii, 1929-1939. vol. 1-9.11.

MOSKVA. ENTSIKLOPEDIIA. 1980.

PEDAGOGICHESKAIA ENTSIKLOPEDIIA. Moscow, Rabotnik prosveshcheniia, 1927-1930. 3 vols.

PEDAGOGICHESKAIA ENTSIKLOPEDIIA. 1964-1968. 4 vols.

RABOCHAIA ENTSIKLOPEDIIA. 1928-1980 GODY. Leningrad. Lenizdat, 1982.

RUSSKII IAZYK. ENTSIKLOPEDIIA. Moscow, Russkii iazyk, 1980.

SOVETSKAIA ISTORICHESKAIA ENTSIKLOPEDIIA. 1961-1976. 16 vols.

SOVETSKAIA VOENNAIA ENTSIKLOPEDIIA. Moscow, Voenizdat, 1976-1980. 8 vols.

TEATRAL'NAIA ENTSIKLOPEDIIA. 1961-1967. 5 vols. and supplement.

TRUDOVOE PRAVO. ENTSIKLOPEDICHESKII SLOVAR'. 1959.

VOENNAIA ENTSIKLOPEDIIA. Moscow,I.D. Sytin, 1911-1915. 18 vols.

VOENNYI ENTSIKLOPEDICHESKII SLOVAR'. Moskva, Voenizdat, 1983.

There are also encyclopedias for republics.

5.2.2.3. English language subject encyclopedias: a selection

The following encyclopedias are being published by Acadamic International Press in Gulf Breeze, Fla.:

THE MODERN ENCYCLOPEDIA OF RUSSIAN AND SOVIET HISTORY (MERSH). J.L. Wieczynski, ed. Vol. 1, 1976-

THE MODERN ENCYCLOPEDIA OF RUSSIAN AND SOVIET LITERATURE (MERSL). H.B. Weber, ed. Vol. 1, 1977-

THE MILITARY-NAVAL ENCYCLOPEDIA OF RUSSIA AND THE SOVIET UNION. D.L. Jones, ed. Vol. 1, 1978-

5.3. Biographical sources

5.3.1. Bibliography

Kaufman, I.M. RUSSKIE BIOGRAFICHESKIE I BIO-BIBLIOGRAFICHESKIE SLOVARI. 2nd ed. Moscow, Gos. izd. kul'turno-prosvetitel'noi literatury, 1955.

5.3.2. General sources

Institute for the Study of the USSR, München. BIOGRAPHIC DIRECTORY OF THE USSR. New York, Scarecrow Press, 1958.

EZHEGODNIK. BOL'SHAIA SOVETSKAIA ENTSIKLOPEDIA. Moscow, Sovetskaia entsiklopedia, 1957-

Heiliger, W. SOVIET AND CHINESE PERSONALITIES. Lanham, Md., University Press of America, 1980.

KLEINE SLAVISCHE BIOGRAPHIE. Wiesbaden, Otto Harrassowitz, 1958.

Krassovsky, D. BIOGRAPHICAL INDEX OF SLAVIC MEN AND WOMEN OF LETTERS, SCIENCE, ART, POLITICS, ARMY, NAVY, ETC. Stanford University, 1943-44. 8 parts and index. Typescipt.

Lewytzkyj, B. and Stroynowski, J. WHO'S WHO IN THE SOCIALIST COUNTRIES... New York, K.G. Saur, 1978.

Lewytzkyj, B. THE SOVIET POLITICAL ELITE: BRIEF BIOGRAPHIES. Stanford, Hoover Institution, 1970.

Lewytzkyj, B., ed. WHO'S WHO IN THE SOVIET UNION... New York, K.G. Saur, 1984.

PORTRAITS OF PROMINENT U.S.S.R. PERSONALITIES. München, Institute for the study of the U.S.S.R. 1966-

PROMINENT PERSONALITIES IN THE U.S.S.R. Metuchen, N.J., The Scarecrow Press, 1968.

U.S.S.R. FACTS AND FIGURES ANNUAL. Gulf Breeze, Fla., Academic International Press, 1977-

Simmons, G. SOVIET LEADERS. New York, Crowell, 1967.

"Sources of Biographic Information on Soviet Officials". RADIO LIBERTY RESEARCH, 29 March, 1977; 1-4.

YEARBOOK ON INTERNATIONAL COMMUNIST AFFAIRS. Stanford, Hoover Institution, 1966.

WHO'S WHO IN THE U.S.S.R., 1965-1966. New York, Scarecrow Press, 1966.

de Boer S.P., et al.BIOGRAPHICAL DICTIONARY OF DISSIDENTS IN THE SOVIET UNION. The Hague, M. Nijhoff, 1982.

5.3.3. Government and Political Leaders

Central Intelligence Agency. DIRECTORY OF SOVIET OFFICIALS, Vol. I: NATIONAL ORGANIZATIONS. Washington, D.C., GPO, 1978.

DIRECTORY OF SOVIET OFFICIALS. Vol. II: RSFSR ORGANIZATIONS. Washington, D.C., GPO, 1980.

DIRECTORY OF SOVIET OFFICIALS. Vol. III: UNION REPUBLICS. Washington, D.C., GPO, 1979.

DIRECTORY OF U.S.S.R. MINISTRY OF DEFENSE AND ARMED FORCES OFFICIALS. Washington, D.C., GPO, 1980.
All CIA directories give job, name, date of position, date of birth, and addresses of agencies. Latest update in 1984.

DIRECTORY OF U.S.S.R. MINISTRY OF FOREIGN AFFAIRS OFFICIALS. Washington, D.C., GPO, 1980.

CURRENT SOVIET LEADERS. Oakville, Ontario, Mosaic Press, 1975-

Hodnett, G. and Oogareff, V. LEADERS OF THE SOVIET REPUBLICS, 1955-1972. Canberra, Australian Nat'l. Univ., 1973. Same for 1971-1980. Canberra, 1980.

SOWJETUNION INTERN HANDBUCH DER FÜHRUNGSGREMIEN. N. Nor-Mešek, W. Rieper, eds. Frankfurt am Main, Institut fur Sowjet-Studien:

Vol. XIII. A.B. DIE MITGLIEDER DES ZENTRALKOMITEES DER KPDSU GEWÄHLT AUF DEM XXVI. PARTEIKONGRESS. 1983. 2 vols.

Vol. XIV. DIE KANDIDATEN DES ZENTRALKOMITEES DER KPDSU GEWÄHLT AUF DEM XXVI PARTEIKONGRESS. 1983.

Vol. XV. DIE ZENTRALE REVISIONSKOMMISSION DER KPDSU GEWÄHLT AUF DEM XXVI PARTEIKONGRESS. 1982 (sic).

5.3.4. Writers

Matsuev, N.I. RUSSKIE SOVETSKIE PISATELI. MATERIALY DLIA BIOGRAFICHESKOGO SLOVARIA. 1917-1967. Moskva, Sovetskii Pisatel', 1981.

Kasack, W. LEXIKON DER RUSSISCHEN LITERATUR AB 1917. Stuttgart, Kroener, 1976.

SOVETSKIE PISATELI. AVTOBIOGRAFII. B.Ia. Brainina, E.F. Nikitina, eds. Moscow, Khudozhestvennaia literatura, 1959-1972. 4 vols.

SPRAVOCHNIK SOIUZA PISATELEI SSSR NA... Moscow, Sovetskii pisatel'. (Latest edition 1981).

Butrin, M. PISATELI-LAUREATY PREMII SSSR I SOIUZNYKH RESPUBLIK. SPRAVOCHNIK. 2nd. ed. L'vov, Vyshcha shkola, 1982.

See also bio-bibliographic dictionaries for writers associated with republics, regions or cities, e.g.,

Bakhtin, V.S., Lur'e, A.N. PISATELI LENINGRADA. BIOBIBLIOGRAFICHESKII SPRAVOCHNIK. 1934-1981. Leningrad, 1982.

5.3.5. Scholars and scientists

AKADEMIIA NAUK SSSR. PERSONAL'NYI SOSTAV. DEISTVITEL'NYE CHLENY, CHLENY-KORRESPONDENTY, POCHETNYE CHLENY, INOSTRANNYE CHLENY. Moscow, Nauka, 1974:Kn.1. 1724-1917.
Kn.2. 1917-1974.

AKADEMIIA NAUK SSSR. SIBIRSKOE OTDELENIE. PERSONAL'NYI SOSTAV. 1957-1982. Novosibirsk, Nauka, 1982.

Korneev, S.G. SOVETSKIE UCHENYE, POCHETNYE CHLENY NAUCHNYKH ORGANIZATSII ZARUBEZHNYKH STRAN. Moscow, Nauka 1981.

Central Intelligence Agency. DIRECTORY OF SOVIET OFFICIALS, VOL. IV: SCIENCE AND EDUCATION. Washington, D.C., GPO, 1980.

MATERIALY K BIBLIOGRAFII UCHENYKH SSSR. Moscow, AN SSSR, 1949-. (for issues published see KATALOG KNIG IZDATEL'STVA NAUKA, 1945- .)

NAUKA I NAUCHNYE RABOTNIKI SSSR. (The author examined the following volumes:)
II. NAUCHNYE UCHREZHDENIIA LENINGRADA. Leningrad, 1926.
IV. NAUCHNYE RABOTNIKI MOSKVY. Leningrad, 1930.

VI. NAUCHNYE RABOTNIKI SSSR BEZ MOSKVY I LENINGRADA. Leningrad, 1928.

Sokolovskaia, Z.K. 300 BIOGRAFII UCHENYKH: O KNIGAKH SERII "NAUCHNO-BIOGRAFICHESKAIA LITERATURA". 1959-1980. BIOBIBLIOGRAFICHESKII SPRAVOCHNIK. Moscow, Nauka, 1982.

Melinskaya, S.I. SOVIET SCIENCE 1917-1970. Part 1. ACADEMY OF SCIENCES OF THE USSR. P.K. Urban, A.I. Lebed, eds. Metuchen, N.J., Scarecrow Press, 1971-.

WHO'S WHO IN SOVIET SCIENCE AND TECHNOLOGY. New York, Telberg, 1960.

WHO'S WHO IN SOVIET SOCIAL SCIENCES, HUMANITIES, ART AND GOVERNMENT. New York, Telberg, 1961.

Additional bibliographic data can be found in the histories of Academies of Sciences and lists of works and dissertations produced by the Academy of Sciences and the major universities.

5.3.6. Artists

SPRAVOCHNIK CHLENOV SOIUZA KHUDOZHNIKOV SSSR: PO SOSTOIANIIU NA...(latest 1977)

5.3.7. Film and Stage personalities

Birkos, A.S. SOVIET CINEMA: DIRECTORS AND FILMS. Hamden, Conn., Archon, 1976.

Chernenko, R.D. 20 REZHISSERSKIKH BIOGRAFII. Moscow, Iskusstvo, 1978.

Dolmatovskaia G.E., Shilova I. WHO'S WHO IN SOVIET CINEMA. Moscow, Progress, 1979 (a translation of 1978 Russian edition).

Iakovlev, M. MASTERA BOL'SHOGO TEATRA: NARODNYE ARTISTY SSSR. Moscow, Sovetskii kompozitor,1976.

STSENARISTY SOVETSKOGO KHUDOZHESTVENNOGO KINO, 1917-1967. SPRAVOCHNIK. Moscow, Iskusstvo, 1967.

SPRAVOCHNIK SOIUZA KINEMATOGRAFOV SSSR. (Latest 1981).

For additional sources, see:

RADIO LIBERTY RESEARCH, March 29, 1977.

5.3.8. Musicians

Bernandt, G.B., Dolzhanskii, A. SOVETSKIE KOMPOZITORY. KRATKII BIOGRAFICHESKII SPRAVOCHNIK. Moscow, Sovetskii kompozitor, 1957.

Bernandt, G.B. KTO PISAL O MUZYKE. BIOBIBLIOGRAFICHESKII SLOVAR' MUZYKAL'NYKH KRITIKOV I LITS, PISAVSHIKH O MUZYKE V DOREVOLIUTSIONNOI ROSSII I SSSR. Moscow, Sovetskii kompositor, 1971-

5.4. Linguistic dictionaries

See part II. 4.8.

5.5. Dictionary of Pseudonyms

Masanov, Iu. F. SLOVAR' PSEVDONIMOV RUSSKIKH PISATELEI, UCHENYKH I OBSHCHESTVENNYKH DEIATELEI. Moscow, Vsesoiuznaia Knizhnaia Palata, 1956-1960. 4 vols.

5.6. Statistics

5.6.1. Bibliographies

5.6.1.1. Russian Pre-1917

Zaionchkovskii, op. cit., is the major reference source.

Chernevskii, P.O. UKAZATEL' MATERIALOV DLIA ISTORII TORGOVLI, PROMYSHLENNOSTI I FINANSOV V PREDELAKH ROSSIISKOI IMP. OT DREVNIKH VREMEN DO KONTSA XVIII ST. St. Petersburg, 1883.

Karavaev, V.F. BIBLIOGRAFICHESKII OBZOR ZEMSKOI STATISTICHESKOI I OTSENOCHNOI LITERATURY SO VREMENI UCHREZHDENIIA ZEMSTV, 1864-1903, St. Petersburg, 1906-1913, vyp. 1-2.

Karataev, S.I. BIBLIOGRAFIIA FINANSOV, PROMYSHLENNOSTI I TORGOVLI... (s 1714 po 1879). St. Petersburg, 1880.

Mezhov, V.I. LITERATURA RUSSKOI GEOGRAFII, ETNOGRAFII I STATISTIKI, 1859-1880., St. Petersburg, 1861-1883, 9 vol., 1st vol. published as BIBLIOGRAFICHESKII UKAZATEL' VYSHEDSHIKH V ROSSII KNIG I STATEI PO CHASTI GEOGRAFII...

"Sistematicheskii ukazatel' izdanii Tsentr. Statisticheskogo Komiteta s 1863- goda po 30 aprelia 1913 goda" in: IUBILEINYI SBORNIK TSENTR. STATISTICHESKOGO KOMITETA MINISTERSTVA VNUTRENNIKH DEL: 1863-1913, St. Petersburg, 1913.

Grigor'ev, V.N. PREDMETNYI UKAZATEL' MATERIALOV V ZEMSKO-STATISTICHESKIKH TRUDAKH S 1860KH GODOV PO 1917. Moscow, 1926-27. 2 vols.

Stepanov, V.P. BIBLIOGRAFICHESKII OBZOR STATISTICHESKIKH IZDANII. St. Petersburg, 1895-1897, vyp, 1-2, (includes statistics published by the Ministerstvo vnutrennikh del and Ministerstvo finansov).

5.6.1.2. Soviet

Mashikhin, E.A., Simchera, V.M. STATISTICHESKIE PUBLIKATSII V SSSR. BIBLIOGRAFICHESKII UKAZATEL'. 1918-1972. Moscow, Statistika, 1975.

KNIGI IZDATEL'STVA "STATISTIKA". 1971-1975 GG. BIBLIOGRAFICHESKII UKAZATEL'. Moscow, Statistika, 1976-

5.6.2. Selected Russian statistical publications

STATISTICHESKII VREMENNIK ROSSIISKOI IMPERII. Ser. 1-3, vyp. 1-25, 1866-1890.

VREMENNIK TSENTR. STATISTICHESKOGO KOMITETA

MINISTERSTVA VNUTRENNIKH DEL, No. 1-52, 1888-1903.

STATISTIKA ROSSIISKOI IMPERII, No. 1-95, 1887-1917.

5.6.3. Selected Soviet statistical publications

Issued by:

Tsentral'noe statisticheskoe upravlenie:
RSFSR V TSIFRAKH V...
MOSKVA V TSIFRAKH ...
SSSR V TSIFRAKH
NARODNOE KHOZIAISTVO SSSR
NARODNOE KHOZIAISTVO RSFSR
NASELENIE SSSR, 1974-
SSSR I SOIUZNYE RESPUBLIKI V...
TRUD V SSSR, 1975-
VNESHNIAIA TORGOVLIA SSSR V...

NARODNOE KHOZIAISTVO SSSR. 1922-1982: IUBILEINYI STATISTICHESKII EZHEGODNIK TSSU SSSR. Moscow, Finansy i statistika, 1982.

Sovet Ekonomicheskoi Vzaimopomoshchi. Sekretariat: STATISTICHESKII EZHEGODNIK STRAN CHLENOV SEV (Soveta Ekonomicheskoi vzaimopomoshchi).

Vsesoiuznaia Knizhnaia Palata: PECHAT' SSSR V... GODU. STATISTICHESKII SBORNIK.

For regional statistics issued on the sixtieth anniversary of the Soviet State see:

Zalewski W. "Reference Materials in Russian-Soviet Area Studies 1976-1977". RUSSIAN REVIEW 2, 1978: 217-218 (not comprehensive).

See also:

NASELENIE SSSR. SPRAVOCHNIK. Moscow, Politizdat, 1983.

5.6.4. Histories of statistics

Gozulov, A.I. OCHERKI ISTORII OTECHESTVENNOI STATISTIKI. Moscow, Statistika, 1972.

Livshits, F.D. SOVETSKAIA STATISTIKA ZA POLVEKA: 1917-1967 G. Moscow, Statistika, 1972.

5.6.5. Western statistics on the Soviet Union

When using Western statistics pertaining to Soviet affairs, the source of the data must be determined. The source is usually stated in the preface.

5.6.5.1. Bibliographies

Walker, G.P.M. ed. OFFICIAL PUBLICATIONS OF THE SOVIET UNION AND EASTERN EUROPE 1945-1980. A SELECTED ANNOTATED BIBLIOGRAPHY. London-New York, Mansell, 1982.

Gillula, J.W. BIBLIOGRAPHY OF REGIONAL STATISTICAL HANDBOOKS IN THE USSR. 2nd ed. Washington D.C., Foreign Demographic Analysis Division. Bureau of the Census, 1980.

5.6.5.2. Selected statistical sources

Clarke, R.A., Matko, D.J.I. SOVIET ECONOMIC FACTS 1917-1981. 2nd ed. London, Macmillan, 1983.

Lewytzkyi, B. THE SOVIET UNION - FACTS, FIGURES, AND DATA. München, K.G. Saur, 1979.

Shoup, P.S. THE EAST EUROPEAN AND SOVIET DATA HANDBOOK - POLITICAL, SOCIAL, AND DEVELOPMENTAL INDICATORS. 1945-1975. New York, Columbia University Press, 1981.

USSR FACTS AND FIGURES ANNUAL. Gulf Breeze, Fla, Academic International Press, 1977-

Also:

United Nations. Department of Economic and Social Affairs. Statistical Office. STATISTICAL YEARBOOK; DEMOGRAPHIC YEARBOOK.

Unesco. STATISTICAL YEARBOOK.

5.7. Geographic sources

5.7.1. Bibliographies

Shibanov, F.A. UKAZATEL' KARTOGRAFICHESKOI LITERATURY, VYSHEDSHEI V ROSSII S 1800 PO 1917 GOD. Leningrad, Universitet, 1961.

Zakharova, A.S. SOVETSKIE ATLASY, 1965-1982. BIBLIOGRAFICHESKII UKAZATEL'. Moscow, MPB, 1983.

KARTOGRAFICHESKAIA LETOPIS' (see national bibliography)

Kaufman, I.M. GEOGRAFICHESKIE SLOVARI. BIBLIOGRAFIIA. Moscow, Kniga, 1964.

Boldov, V.B. "Geograficheskie slovari. Bibliograficheskii ukazatel' slovarei, izdannykh v SSSR 1917-1971 gg." GEOGRAFICHESKII SBORNIK 5, 1975: 211-223.

Also general guides:

Zaionchkovskii, P.A. SPRAVOCHNIKI...

Shapiro,A.L. ISTORIIA SSSR..., pp.174-191.

Maichel, K. GUIDE TO RUSSIAN REFERENCE BOOKS. Vol. II. HISTORY,AUXILIARY SCIENCES, ETNOGRAPHY, AND GEOGRAPHY. Stanford, Hoover Institution, 1964: 189-227. (HOOVER INSTITUTION BIBLIOGRAPHICAL SERIES, XVIII).

5.7.2. Non-bibliographic sources

Semenov (Tian-Shanskii), P.P. ROSSIIA, POLNOE GEOGRAFICHESKOE OPISANIE NASHEGO OTECHESTVA. St.Petersburg, 1899-1913. 19 vols. (incomplete).

GEOGRAFICHESKO-STATISTICHESKII SLOVAR' ROSSIISKOI IMPERII. St. Petersburg, 1863-1885. 5 vols.

SOVETSKII SOIUZ. GEOGRAFICHESKOE OPISANIE V 22-KH TOMAKH. Moscow, Mysl', 1967-

Vasmer, M. RUSSISCHES GEOGRAPHISCHES NAMENBUCH. Wiesbaden, O. Harrassowitz, 1964-

United States Board on Geographic Names. USSR OFFICIAL STANDARD NAMES. GAZETTEER. No. 43. 2nd ed. Washington, D.C.. 1970. 7 vols.

SSSR. ADMINISTRATIVNO - TERRITORIAL'NOE DELENIE SOIUZNYCH RESPUBLIK NA 1 IANVARIA... Latest edition: Moscow, [Izvestia], 1983. Revised periodically.

Ariskevich, N.P., et al. SLOVAR' GEOGRAFICHESKIKH NAZVANII SSSR. 2nd ed. Moscow, Nedra, 1983.

See also encyclopedias.

5.8. Directories

5.8.1. Bibliography

Zaionchkovskii, P.A. SPRAVOCHNIKI...

Walker, G.P.M. OFFICIAL SOVIET PUBLICATIONS...

5.8.2. Business

THE RUSSIAN YEARBOOK. London, 1911-1916.

RUSSIAN ALMANAC. London, Eyre and Spottiswoode, Ltd., 1919.

Santalov, A.A., Segal, L. SOVIET UNION YEARBOOK. London, George Allen & Unwin, Ltd., 1930.

BUSINESSMAN'S MOSCOW. HANDBOOK AND DIRECTORY OF SOVIET FOREIGN BUSINESS COMMUNITIES IN THE USSR. DELOVAIA MOSKVA. SPRAVOCHNIK SOVETSKIKH I INOSTRANNYKH DELOVYKH KRUGOV V SSSR. [Moscow, Vneshtorgreklama, 1984].

U.S. INFORMATION MOSCOW. A COMPLETE REFERENCE HANDBOOK TO MOSCOW AND THE USSR. A.P. Friedland, ed. Mountain View, CA, Dime's Group, Inc., 1978- Updated annually.

See also Part II. 5.8.1.

5.8.3. Academic Institutions

See Part I. 5.3.5.

THE WORLD OF LEARNING.

There are histories of the various academies of sciences, universities and other institutions but there is no directory of academic institutions.

For Western sources see:

GUIDE DU SLAVISTE. Paris, Institute d'Études Slaves, 1971-

Sendich, M. "Russian and Slavic Programs and Faculty in United States and Canadian Colleges: 1982-1983". RUSSIAN LANGUAGE JOURNAL 37 (126-127, Winter-Spring) 1983:177-209.

5.8.4. City directories

Soviet telephone books are difficult to obtain. However, some directories of institutions have been published for various cities. Identification of these is not always easy since not all are registered even in EZHEGODNIK KNIGI. The samples below are intended to note their existence:

GOROD IVANOVO. KRATKAIA ADRESNO-SPRAVOCHNAIA KNIGA.

Ivanovo, Rabochii krai, 1973.

LENINGRAD. KRATKAIA ADRESNO-SPRAVOCHNAIA KNIGA. Leningrad, Leninzdat, 1973.

MOSKVA. KRATKAIA ADRESNO-SPRAVOCHNAIA KNIGA. Moscow, Moskovskii rabochii, 1965.

5.9. Current events

BOL'SHAIA SOVETSKAIA ENTSIKLOPEDIIA. 2nd ed. EZHEGODNIK, 1957-

KUL'TURNAIA ZHIZN' V SSSR... KHRONIKA. Moscow, Nauka, 1975-
to date published were volumes for:
1917-1927. 1975
1928-1940. 1976.
1941-1950. 1977.
1951-1965. 1979.
1966-1977. 1981.

See also Western sources such as PUBLIC AFFAIRS INFORMATION SERVICE and others.

5.10. Political guides, events, data

Sworakowski, W. WORLD COMMUNISM. A HANDBOOK. Stanford, Hoover Institution, 1965, continued by

Staar, R., ed. YEARBOOK ON INTERNATIONAL COMMUNIST AFFAIRS. Stanford, Hoover Institution, 1966-

Staar, R. COMMUNIST REGIMES IN EASTERN EUROPE. 4th ed. Stanford, Hoover Institution, 1982.

POLITICHESKIE PARTII. SPRAVOCHNIK. Moscow, Politizdat, 1981. (world coverage).

KPSS. SPRAVOCHNIK. 5th ed. Moscow, Politizdat, 1983.

SOVETY NARODNYKH DEPUTATOV. SPRAVOCHNIK. A.I. Lukianov, et al., eds. Moscow, Politizdat, 1984.

PART II

SUBJECT (OTRASLEVYE) BIBLIOGRAPHIES

Area study bibliographies have developed their own bibliographic universe, which is based and dependent on general bibliographies. They correspond to the unique needs of the disciplines they serve, the predominant publishing formats, and the institutions which sponsor or guide the research and promote the publications, as well as store them (such as libraries and museums). An understanding of all these factors aids the bibliographic search.

Subject bibliographies are usually compiled on the basis of general bibliographies and are further expanded through original research. Consequently Part II is founded on Part I and the sources listed there will still play a crucial role for subject searches. The importance of Kandel''s bibliography of bibliographies of bibliographies, BIBLIOGRAFIIA SOVETSKOI BIBLIOGRAFII, other series of national bibliography, and several other sources must be reiterated.

Subject bibliographies range from general, covering a whole discipline, to those covering minute issues. They appear as books, or are attached to monographs (priknizhnye) or articles (pristateinye), and sometimes even are "hidden" in footnotes. While the broad subject bibliographies are prepared mainly by major institutions, specialized topics remain in hands of scholars and individual bibliographers. Obviously, the narrower the specialization, the more difficult the bibliographic search and the more complex the bibliographic technique. In the final account the search must often leave the published sources and turn to personal relations between scholars bound by a common interest for guidance, leads to archival resources, or information about research in progress.

Each field has its own history of bibliography. These histories in most cases have not yet been written. Those interested, however, will be able to find quite extensive, although scattered, data through Part I. 1-3. Moreover, prefaces to major bibliographies will be helpful. They should be read not only as keys to understanding of the work itself, but also as introductions to the bibliographic network.

Bibliographic works done before and after the Revolution differ significantly. Most of these differences are obvious from the titles listed in Part I. The issues are not only related to different ideological principles but also to the size of the published output. Before the Revolution, especially before the 1870's, individual bibliographers still could assess the whole publishing scene. Such persons as Vladimir I. Mezhov, Augusta V. Mez'er, and Semen A. Vengerov created bibliographies of giant proportions by amassing files reaching as many as a million entries. Today their work alleviates to some extent the need for general nineteenth century bibliographies in selected subject areas. And yet their efforts were haphazard, unfinished, and bibliographically incomplete.

The size of the publishing output in the USSR required an institutionalized approach to bibliographic work. Still the results of bibliographic endeavors in various disciplines are uneven. Significant progress has been made in providing bibliographies of bibliographies covering pre-revolutionary Russia as well as the Soviet period. Several very specialized bibliographies cross the 1917 borders. Better work has been done in pre- revolutionary literature than in pre-1917 history and the social sciences. There are good current bibliographic services. Efforts are made to produce general bibliographies in subject areas covering all Soviet imprints (1917 and after). These are anchored in major libraries and bibliographic institutions, as well as in institutions with specialized missions, such as museums of a writer, regional libraries, etc.

1. Soviet bibliographic institutions

In the Soviet Union numerous information centers search literature in the disciplines of their responsibility and produce series of express information, reviews, digests, abstracts, and bibliographies. Major libraries, both central and regional, participate in these activities. The most concentrated effort, however, is made by the Vsesoiuznyi Institut Nauchnoi i Tekhnicheskoi Informatsii (VINITI) and the Institut Nauchnoi Informatsii po Obshchestvennym Naukam (INION) both in Moscow. The former deals with science and technology (and as such is out of our scope of interest), the latter with the social sciences and humanities.

1.1. Institut Nauchnoi Informatsii po Obshchestvennym Naukam at the USSR Academy of Sciences (INION). Formerly Fundamental'naia Biblioteka po Obshchestvennym Naukam (FBON).

Early publications by FBON are listed in:

Barykina, O.A., Bykova, N.M. "Opublikovannye raboty FBON (1923-1959 gg.)." FUNDAMENTAL'NAIA BIBLIOTEKA OBSHCHESTVENNYKH NAUK: IZ OPYTA RABOTY ZA 40 LET. SBORNIK STATEI. Moscow, 1960: 288-313.

INION was formed in 1969. Information about its main academic thrust can be obtained from the book by its director V.A. Vinogradov, OBSHCHESTVENNYE NAUKI I INFORMATSIIA. Moscow, Nauka, 1978. Its activities can be grouped in the following categories:

the collection of papers (REFERATIVNYE SBORNIKI) (beyond our scope);

abstracts (REFERATIVNYE ZHURNALY);

retrospective bibliographies which are prepared by INION independently or in cooperation with other major libraries and institutions in the USSR covering imprints issued since 1917;

current bibliographies, prepared either by INION independently or in collaboration with information centers or Academies of Sciences in other East European countries. This cooperative body, called Mezhdunarodnaia Informatsionnaia Sistema po Obshchestvennym Naukam (MISON), over which INION presides, was formed in 1976.

INION publishes abstracts in the following series:

OBSHCHESTVENNYE NAUKI V SSSR:
- PROBLEMY NAUCHNOGO KOMMUNIZMA;
- EKONOMIKA;
- FILOSOFSKIE NAUKI;
- GOSUDARSTVO I PRAVO;
- ISTORIIA;
- LITERATUROVEDENIE;
- IAZYKOZNANIE.

OBSHCHESTVENNYE NAUKI ZA RUBEZHOM:
- VOSTOKOVEDENIE I AFRIKANISTIKA;
- PROBLEMY NAUCHNOGO KOMMUNIZMA;
- EKONOMIKA;
- FILOSOFIIA I SOTSIOLOGIIA;
- GOSUDARSTVO I PRAVO;
- ISTORIIA;
- LITERATUROVEDENIE;
- IAZYKOZNANIE;
- NAUKOVEDENIE.

Current bibliographic registration began in 1947. The titles of some series have changed. Now there are 29 series divided into three main parts. Together the service covers about 110,000 Soviet and 140,000 foreign titles annually. The monthly issues are not cumulated. These sources together with the national bibliography serve as a basis for retrospective subject bibliographies.

The current bibliographic series has a generic title, BIBLIOGRAFICHESKII UKAZATEL' which is further subdivided into:

1. NOVAIA SOVETSKAIA LITERATURA PO OBSHCHESTVENNYM NAUKAM:
   GOSUDARSTVO I PRAVO;
   ISTORIIA. ARKHEOLOGIIA. ETNOGRAFIIA;
   LITERATUROVEDENIE;
   NAUKOVEDENIE;
   FILOSOFSKIE NAUKI;
   EKONOMIKA;
   IAZYKOZNANIE;
   NAUCHNYI KOMMUNIZM.

2. NOVAIA INOSTRANNAIA LITERATURA PO OBSHCHESTVENNYM NAUKAM:
   GOSUDARSTVO I PRAVO;
   ISTORIIA. ARKHEOLOGIIA. ETNOGRAFIIA;
   LITERATUROVEDENIE;
   NAUKOVEDENIE;
   FILOSOFIIA I SOTSIOLOGIIA;
   EKONOMIKA;
   IAZYKOZNANIE.

3. NOVAIA SOVETSKAIA I INOSTRANNAIA LITERATURA PO OBSHCHESTVENNYM NAUKAM:
   BLIZHNII I SREDNII VOSTOK. AFRIKA;
   VENGERSKAIA NARODNAIA RESPUBLIKA;
   GERMANSKAIA DEMOKRATICHESKAIA RESPUBLIKA;
   EVROPEISKIE SOTSIALISTICHESKIE STRANY. OBSHCHIE PROBLEMY;
   MEZHDUNARODNOE RABOCHEE DVIZHENIE;
   NARODNAIA RESPUBLIKA BOLGARIIA;
   POL'SKAIA NARODNAIA RESPUBLIKA;
   PROBLEMY ATEIZMA I RELIGII;
   PROBLEMY SLAVIANOVEDENIIA I BALKANISTIKI;
   SOTSIALISTICHESKAIA RESPUBLIKA RUMYNIIA;
   SOTSIALISTICHESKAIA FEDERATIVNAIA RESPUBLIKA IUGOSLAVIIA;
   STRANY AZII I AFRIKI. OBSHCHIE PROBLEMY;
   CHEKHOSLOVATSKAIA SOTSIALISTICHESKAIA RESPUBLIKA;
   IUZHNAIA I IUGO-VOSTOCHNAIA AZIIA. DAL'NII VOSTOK.

The retrospective bibliographies usually begin with current registration and gradually close the gap from 1917 to present. It may be presumed that INION aims to produce crucial subject bibliographies which ideally would cover the whole Soviet period. Examples of major bibliographies prepared either in cooperation with other libraries or by INION alone are: ISTORIIA SSSR. UKAZATEL' SOVETSKOI LITERATURY. 1917-1952- ; SOVETSKOE LITERATUROVEDENIE I KRITIKA... 1917-1962- ; SLAVIANSKOE IAZYKOZNANIE... 1918-1960- ; OBSHCHIE IAZYKOZNANIE... 1918-1962- . (For full bibliographic data see subject sections below).

The listing below shows the breadth of INION's retrospective bibliographic activities:

KATALOG DEPONIROVANNYKH RUKOPISEI. OBSHCHESTVENNYE NAUKI. 1963-1975 GG. Moscow, 1976.

SOVMESTNYE NAUCHNYE TRUDY UCHENYKH SOTSIALISTICHESKIKH STRAN V OBLASTI OBSHCHESTVENNYKH NAUK. BIBLIOGRAFICHESKIE MATERIALY (PO FONDAM INION). 1969-1974, Moscow, 1975-

AKTUAL'NYE PROBLEMY METODOLOGII OBSHCHESTVENNYKH NAUK. BIBLIOGRAFICHESKIE MATERIALY. 1965-1977 GG. Moscow, 1978.

SOTSIALISTICHESKII OBRAZ ZHIZNI. UKAZATEL' LITERATURY. 1979 G. Moscow, 1980-

SOCIAL SCIENCES IN THE USSR. ANNOTATED BIBLIOGRAPHY FOR 1981. Moscow, 1983-

SOCIAL SCIENCES IN SOCIALIST COUNTRIES. Vol. 1. SELECTED LITERATURE FROM 1978-1979. Moscow, 1981-

INFORMATSIIA I OBSHCHESTVENNYE NAUKI. UKAZATEL' LITERATURY, OPUBLIKOVANNOI V SSSR. 1972-1977. Moscow, 1977.

SOEDINENNYE SHTATY AMERIKI. UKAZATEL' KNIG I STATEI NA RUSSKOM IAZYKE O SOVREMENNOM POLITICHESKOM POLOZHENII, EKONOMIKE, KUL'TURE, GEOGRAFII I ISTORII SShA. Moscow, 1971-

PROBLEMY NAUKOVEDENIIA. AVTOREFERATY DISSERTATSII. 1965-1977. Moscow, 1979.

NAUKA I NAUCHNO-ISSLEDOVATEL'SKAIA RABOTA V SSSR. LITERATURA, OPUBLIKOVANNAIA V 1917-1925 GG. Moscow, 1981. INION intends to close the gap with earlier published volumes: 1946-1954. Moscow, 1954; 1954-1961. Moscow, 1963. Current coverage: NOVAIA SOVETSKAIA LITERATURA PO OBSHCHESTVENNYM NAUKAM. NAUKOVEDENIE (since 1947; title changed).

VOPROSY METODOLOGII NAUCHNOGO POZNANIIA. ESTESTVENNYE, MATEMATICHESKIE I OBSHCHESTVENNYE NAUKI. UKAZATEL' SOVETSKOI LITERATURY. 1976-. Moscow, 1977-

FILOSOFIIA I KUL'TURA. UKAZATEL' LITERATURY, IZDANNOI V SSSR NA RUSSKOM IAZYKE V 1974-1981 GG. Moscow, 1983.

ISTORIIA RUSSKOI FILOSOFII. UKAZATEL' LITERATURY, IZDANNOI V SSSR NA RUSSKOM IAZYKE V 1917-1967 GG. Moscow, 1967 and continuation for 1968-1977 in 1981.

ISTORIIA ZARUBEZHNOI DOMARKSISTSKOI FILOSOFII. UKAZATEL' LITERATURY, IZDANNOI V SSSR V 1917-1967. Moscow, 1972 and continuation.

SOVREMENNAIA ZARUBEZHNAIA FILOSOFIIA I SOTSIOLOGIIA. UKAZATEL' LITERATURY, IZDANNOI V SSSR V 1973 G. Moscow, 1975-

DIALEKTICHESKII MATERIALIZM. UKAZATEL' LITERATURY, IZDANNOI V SSSR V 1971-1973. Moscow, 1976-

DIALEKTICHESKII MATERIALIZM I SOVREMENNOE ESTESTVOZNANIE. LITERATURA IZDANNAIA V SSSR, 1956-1967. Moscow, 1971.

DIALEKTICHESKII MATERIALIZM I ESTESTVOZNANIE. UKAZATEL' LITERATURY, IZDANNOI V SSSR. Moscow, 1951-

KRITIKA BURZHUAZNOI, REFORMISTSKOI I REVIZIONISTSKOI IDEOLOGII. LITERATURA IZDANNAIA V... GODU. Moscow, 1976-

ISTORICHESKII MATERIALIZM. UKAZATEL' LITERATURY, IZDANNOI V SSSR V 1917-1925 GG. Moscow, 1976- (now published annually with current coverage).

MARKSISTSKO-LENINSKAIA TEORIIA POZNANIIA. UKAZATEL' LITERATURY, IZDANNOI V SSSR NA RUSSKOM IAZYKE,

1956-1972 GG. Moscow, 1974. 3 vols.

MARKSISTSKO-LENINSKAIA ETIKA. UKAZATEL' LITERATURY, IZDANNOI V SSSR. 1972-1973 [and for 1974-1975]. Moscow, 1975-

MARKSIZM-LENINIZM O GLOBAL'NYKH PROBLEMAKH SOVREMENNOSTI. UKAZATEL' SOVETSKOI LITERATURY. 1972-1982 GG. Moscow, 1983.

MARKSIZM-LENINIZM - TEORETICHESKAIA OSNOVA SOVREMENNOGO SOTSIAL'NOGO PROGRESSA. UKAZATEL' REFERATOV INION AN SSSR ZA 1978-1983 GG. Moscow, 1983.

SOTSIOLOGICHESKIE ISSLEDOVANIIA. UKAZATEL' LITERATURY, IZDANNOI V SSSR V GODU. Moscow, 1975-

EKONOMICHESKAIA ISTORIIA. UKAZATEL' SOVETSKOI LITERATURY ZA 1960-1969 GG. Moscow, 1970, and continuation in five year intervals.

NARODNOE KHOZIAISTVO SSSR V 1917-1920 GG. BIBLIOGRAFICHESKII UKAZATEL' KNIZHNOI I ZHURNAL'NOI LITERATURY NA RUSSKOM IAZYKE. 1917-1963 GG. Moscow, 1967. Continued as NARODNOE KHOZIAISTVO SSSR V 1921-1925 GG. UKAZATEL' SOVETSKOI LITERATURY. 1921-1974. Moscow, 1980-1981 4 parts. Part 5, Vyp.1: PROMYSHLENNOST' I STROITEL'STVO was published in 1983. It covers materials published from 1921-1980.

NARODNOE KHOZIAISTVO V SSSR V GODY VELIKOI OTECHESTVENNOI VOINY (IIUN' 1941-MAI 1945 GG). BIBLIOGRAFICHESKII UKAZATEL' KNIZHNOI I ZHURNAL'NOI LITERATURY NA RUSSKOM IAZYKE. 1941-1968. Moscow, 1971.

BIBLIOGRAFIIA PO PROBLEMAM NARODONASELENIIA. SOVETSKAIA I PEREVODNAIA LITERATURA. 1960-1971 GG. Moscow, 1974 continued as BIBLIOGRAFIIA NARODONASELENIIA. 1972-1975 GG. Moscow, 1977 and LITERATURA O NASELENII. BIBLIOGRAFICHESKII UKAZATEL'. 1975-1978 GG. Moscow, 1981.

SLAVIANSKIE KUL'TURY I MIROVOI REVOLIUTSIONNYI PROTSESS. UKAZATEL' LITERATURY. 1970-1981 GG. Moscow, 1982-

POLITICHESKIE NAUKI V SSSR. UKAZATEL' SOVETSKOI LITERATURY. 1975-1979. Moscow, 1979-

SOVETSKOE SLAVIANOVEDENIE. UKAZATEL' LITERATURY O ZARUBEZHNYKH SLAVIANSKIKH STRANAKH. 1918-1960. Moscow, 1963-

Bannikova, N.P., et al. VZAIMOSVIAZI I VZAIMO-DEISTVIE NATSIONAL'NYKH LITERATUR. BIBLIOGRAFIIA. 1945-1960. Moscow, 1962. 3 vols. continued by

Libman, V.A., et al. VZAIMOSVIAZI I VZAIMODEISTVIE LITERATUR MIRA. BIBLIOGRAFIIA. 1961-1965. Moscow, 1967-
latest issue: 1976-1980. Moscow, 1983. 3 vols. Its vol. 1 is devoted to Russian literature.

OKTIABR' I POD"EM REVOLIUTSIONNOGO DVIZHENIIA V STRANAKH TSENTRAL'NOI I IUGOVOSTOCHNOI EVROPY (1917-1932 GG.). UKAZATEL' LITERATURY. 1966-1981. Moscow, 1983. 2 vols.

KONSTITUTSIIA SSSR V DEISTVII. UKAZATEL' SOVETSKOI LITERATURY. 1977-1983 GG. Moscow, 1983.

The MISON cooperative has prepared the following bibliographies:

RAZVITOE SOTSIALISTICHESKOE OBSHCHESTVO. UKAZATEL' LITERATURY. 1977 G. Moscow, 1979-

EKONOMICHESKOE I NAUCHNO-TEKHNICHESKOE SOTRUDNICHESTVO STRAN-CHLENOV SEV I SFRIu. UKAZATEL' LITERATURY... G. Moscow, 1976-

KRITIKA SOVREMENNOI BURZHUAZNOI IDEOLOGII REFORMIZMA I REVIZIONIZMA. UKAZATEL' LITERATURY. 1973 G.- Moscow, 1976-

KRITIKA SOVREMENNYKH BURZHUAZNYKH I REVIZIONISTI-CHESKIKH TEORII. UKAZATEL' LITERATURY SOTSIALIS-TICHESKIKH STRAN EVROPY. 1976 G. Moscow, 1977-

SOVMESTNYE NAUCHNYE TRUDY UCHENYKH SOTSIALISTI-CHESKIKH STRAN V OBLAST OBSHCHESTVENNYKH NAUK. UKAZATEL' LITERATURY. 1981-1982 GG. Moscow, 1983-

1.2. Informatsionnyi Tsentr po Problemam Kul'tury i Iskusstva

This Center is located at the Lenin Public Library in Moscow under the patronage of the Ministry of Culture. It began its activities in 1973. It issues:

bibliographic series (BIBLIOGRAFICHESKAIA INFORMATSIIA);

collections of papers (NAUCHNYE REFERATIVNYE SBORNIKI);

abstracts (OBZORNAIA INFORMATSIIA); and

research reports (EKSPRESS-INFORMATSIIA).

In the three latter categories there are the following series:

KUL'TURNO-PROSVETITEL'NAIA RABOTA;

MUZEEVEDENIE I OKHRANA PAMIATNIKOV;

MUZYKA;

OBSHCHIE PROBLEMY KUL'TURY I KUL'TURNOGO STROITEL'-STVA;

TEATR.

In addition to those within the REFERATIVNYE SBORNIKI series there is also

BIBLIOTEKOVEDENIE I BIBLIOGRAFOVEDENIE.

The most important for bibliographic work is the series BIBLIOGRAFICHESKAIA INFORMATSIIA. Within this service the following series are prepared:

IZOBRAZITEL'NOE ISKUSSTVO;

MUZEEVEDENIE I OKHRANA PAMIATNIKOV;

MUZYKA;

TEATR. This series changed in 1983 into

ZRELISHCHNYE ISKUSSTVA which incorporated "Tanets", "Tsirk", and "Estrada". These subjects were published within MUZYKA and TEATR during 1975-1982.

KUL'TURNO-PROSVETITEL'NAIA RABOTA. SAMODEIATEL'NOE TVORCHESTVO;

KUL'TURNO-PROSVETITEL'NAIA RABOTA. NARODNOE TVORCHESTVO;

STROITEL'STVO I ARKHITEKTURA (several series), 1982- ;

OBSHCHIE VOPROSY ISKUSSTVA, 1982- .

2. History

2.1. Publishing

The Academy of Sciences, the universities, historical societies, committees, and to some extent the pedagogical institutes are the primary centers of research in history. The results of this research are usually published by those institutions through their own publishing houses or in series sponsored by them. Information about research institutions can be obtained from guides, historiographies, Zaionchkovskii's SPRAVOCHNIKI, and bibliographies of publications by these institutions. An example of an important institutional bibliography is:

Kraineva, N.Ia., Pronina, P.V. TRUDY INSTITUTA ISTORII AKADEMII NAUK SSSR. 1936-1965 GG. Moscow, 1968. 4 vols.;
1966-1968 in 1969;
1969-1975 in 1977. 3 vols., by P.V. Pronina.

See also bibliography of bibliographies: G.A. Galvatskikh below.

2.2. Libraries, archives, museums

Information about libraries, archives, and museums can be found in Part I.3.1-3. In history the leading role is played by the Gosudarstvennaia Publichnaia Istoricheskaia Biblioteka RSFSR (GPI). It was founded in Moscow in 1938. The library is not only a part of the national library system, but also a major bibliographic center. As such, information about this library and it activities is of bibliographic importance.

For information about the library see:

Lesiuk, E.T. SBORNIK STATEI IZ OPYTA RABOTY ZA 20 LET. Moscow, [GPI], 1958. Contains a selected bibliography: "Izdaniia Gosudarstvennoi Publichnoi Istoricheskoi Biblioteki za 20 let (1938-1958 gg.)", pp.231-236;

Starokadomskaia, M.K. "40-letie Istoricheskoi biblioteki", VOPROSY ISTORII 12, 1978:177-182.

An important library catalog in progress is

Gol'dberg, A.L., Iakovleva, I.G. DOREVOLIUTSIONNYE IZDANIIA PO ISTORII SSSR V INOSTRANNOM FONDE GOSUDARSTVENNOI PUBLICHNOI BIBLIOTEKI IM. M.E. SATLYKOVA-SHCHEDRINA. SISTEMATICHESKII UKAZATEL'. Vypusk 1, Leningrad, 1982.

It expands the coverage of the more general catalog of the same library, namely:

CATALOGUE DE LA SECTION DES RUSSICA OU ÉCRITS SUR LA RUSSIE EN LANGUES ÉTRANGÈRES. St.Petersburg, Bibliothèque Imperiale Publique de St. Petersburg, 1873. 2 vols.

An example of museum holdings is:

Bakst, E.I., et al. PUTEVODITEL' PO FONDAM LICHNOGO PROISKHOZHDENIIA OTDELA PIS'MENNYKH ISTOCHNIKOV GOSUDARSTVENNOGO ISTORICHESKOGO MUZEIA. Moscow, 1967.

Major guides to archival collections, regardless of the type of repository in which these collections are housed, offer introductions dealing with history, holdings, and use of the collections.

2.3. Textbooks, guides, bibliographies of bibliographies

The crucial source from which every systematic bibliographic search must begin is:

Glavatskikh, G.A., et al. ISTORIIA SSSR. ANNOTIROVANNYI UKAZATEL' BIBLIOGRAFICHESKIKH POSOBII, OPUBLIKOVANNYKH NA RUSSKOM IAZYKE S NACHALA XIX V. PO 1982 G. V DVUKH VYPUSKAKH. 3rd ed. Moscow, [GPI], 1983-1984. 2 vols.
Earlier editions which were outdated by the new one, were issued in 1957 and 1966.

Glavatskikh contains introductory essays on the history of the bibliography of history and an outline of the structure of the bibliography of history. The entries are annotated and frequently reviews of bibliographic works are cited.

Earlier guides are:

Maichel, K. GUIDE TO RUSSIAN REFERENCE BOOKS. VOL. II. HISTORY, AUXILIARY SCIENCES, ETHNOGRAPHY, AND GEOGRAPHY. Stanford, Hoover Institution, 1964 (HOOVER INSTITUTION BIBLIOGRAPHICAL SERIES, XVIII).

Shapiro, A.L. BIBLIOGRAFIIA ISTORII SSSR. Moscow, Vysshaia shkola, 1968.

Information about the most recent contributions by Soviet historians to their discipline is registered in

IZUCHENIE OTECHESTVENNOI ISTORII V SSSR MEZHDU XXV I XXVI S"EZDAMI KPSS. Moscow, Nauka, 1982. This contains extensive bibliographic footnotes.

Z.L. Fradkina surveys annually the bibliographies in introductory sections to BIBLIOGRAFIIA SOVETSKOI BIBLIOGRAFII. The bibliographic surveys by W. Zalewski in THE RUSSIAN REVIEW, can be useful. General bibliographies in history discussed below also contain bibliography of bibliographies sections.

2.4. General bibliographies.

By "general bibliographies" in history, we mean bibliographies which cover all aspects and subjects within the field of Russian history. Obviously, no bibliography registers all Russian and Soviet imprints in this field. Russian publications issued prior to 1800 may be found through bibliographies listed in Part I for that period of time. Publications on Russian history which appeared between 1800 and 1917 have been listed in a variety of bibliographies published primarily during the tsarist period. Soviet imprints are being registered retrospectively now. Of course, there are new bibliographies of bibliographies, and a host of narrow subject bibliographies, which contain both pre-revolutionary and Soviet publications.

2.4.1. Pre-1917 imprints

Soviet bibliographers to date have not devoted much attention to the nineteenth century publications dealing with all of Russian history. Consequently, bibliographies published in the nineteenth-century retain their value as the only available general bibliographies for history. The most prominent bibliographer of that time was V.I. Mezhov. A brief discussion of his activities will permit a better understanding of the state of bibliographic sciences in nineteenth-century Russia.

2.4.1.1. Vladimir Izmailovich Mezhov (1830-1894)

Bibliography:

Lisovskii, N.M. "Vladimir Izmailovich Mezhov. Russkii bibliograf", BIBLIOGRAF 2,1894:84-102;

Fradkina, Z.L. V.I. MEZHOV (1830-1984). Moscow, VKP, 1949.

Mezhov was one of the world's greatest bibliographers. He prepared over 100 volumes of bibliography, mainly in the social sciences and humanities. His bibliographic activities began with the registration of current publications in OTECHESTVENNYE ZAPISKI from 1856. This was the year when the official bibliographies in ZHURNAL MINISTERSTVA NARODNOGO PROSVESHCHENIIA ceased. Only two years later the OTECHESTVENNYE ZAPISKI registration was discontinued and Mezhov moved his bibliographic service to ZHURNAL MINISTERSTVA VNUTRENNYKH DEL. As an employee at the Imperial Public Library in St. Petersburg, he initiated current registration of the contents of journals in 1858. This was facilitated by the depository copy received by this library. As result Mezhov developed a large bibliographic file which became a resource for several special bibliographies such as LITERATURA RUSSKOI GEOGRAFII, STATISTIKI I ETNOGRAFII (1859-1880, 9 vols.); "Bibliograficheskii ukazatel' russkoi arkheologicheskoi literatury" in IZVESTIIA IMP. ARKHEOLOGICHESKOGO OBSHCHESTVA (1859-1868); LITERATURA RUSSKOGO

PRAVOVEDENIIA (1859-1866); and LITERATURA RUSSKOI PEDAGOGIKI (1859-1888).

In 1866 Mezhov left the Imperial Library and supported himself entirely on his bibliographic work, thus becoming the first free lance bibliographer in Russia. Of course, he needed wealthy patrons who would commission work. He found them in major book dealers such as Bazunov, Isakov, and Glazunov for whom he prepared bookstore catalogs (see Part I.4.6.1.). He was also hired by the industralist I.M. Sibiriakov for whom he prepared SIBIRSKAIA BIBLIOGRAFIIA (St.Petersburg, 1891-1892. 3 vols.) and later his historical bibliography; and by the military (General'nyi Shtab), which financed BIBLIOGRAFIIA AZII (St. Petersburg, 1891-1892. 3 vols.) and TURKESTANSKII SBORNIK SOCHINENII I STATEI... (St. Petersburg, 1878-1888. 4 vols.). The Ministry of Education supported Mezhov's search of journals and special serials such as GUBERNSKIE VEDOMOSTI. These efforts were published either in the form of current bibliographic registration or in retrospective bibliographies.

Mezhov's predominant interest was in historical bibliography. This was prompted by RUSSKAIA ISTORICHESKAIA BIBLIOGRAFIIA, published annually after 1861 (with coverage beginning with 1855) by the Academy of Sciences and compiled by the brothers Lambin. Mezhov was dissatisfield with the pace at which this bibliography was published (the volume for 1858 appeared as late as 1884), so he moved ahead himself. In 1866 he published LITERATURA RUSSKOI ISTORII ZA 1856-1864 G. VKLIUCHITEL'NO (St. Petersburg, F.S. Sushchintskii, 1866. Vol. 1 only). In this work publications in geography, statistics, ethnography, law, education, literature and linguistics are not included because they appeared as special bibliographies. The use of Mezov's bibliographies is complicated by the fact that he does not incorporate earlier works in his later volumes. His works should be viewed as a unity.

2.4.1.2. Bibliography

The nineteenth-century imprints dealing with Russian history are covered as follows:

(bibliographies are presented in chronological order of the imprints covered rather than in order of the compilation date)

Mezhov, V.I. RUSSKAIA ISTORICHESKAIA BIBLIOGRAFIIA. UKAZATEL' KNIG I STATEI PO RUSSKOI I VSEOBSHCHEI ISTORII I VSPOMOGATEL'NYM NAUKAM ZA 1800-1854. St. Petersburg, I.M. Sibiriakov, 1892-1893. 3 vols.

Lambin, P.P., Lambin, B.P. RUSSKAIA ISTORICHESKAIA BIBLIOGRAFIIA... God. (1855-1864). St.Petersburg Akademiia Nauk, 1861-1884. Annual.

Mezhov, V.I. LITERATURA RUSSKOI ISTORII ZA 1859-1864 G. VKLIUCHITEL'NO. St.Petersburg, F.S. Sushchinskii, 1866.

Mezhov, V.I. RUSSKAIA ISTORICHESKAIA BIBLIOGRAFIIA ZA 1865-1876 VKLIUCHITEL'NO. St. Petersburg, Akademiia Nauk, 1882-1890. 8 vols.

After that date and up to 1917 only short periods, usually annual issues, were published Among them the most important were those published in such journals as RUSSKAIA STARINA, IZVESTIIA ARKHEOLOGICHESKOI KOMISSII. PRIBAVLENIE, and others. Information about this period may be obtained from A.L. Shapiro, op. cit., pp .55-57 and G.A. Glavatskikh, ISTORIIA SSSR, pp. 21-27. ISTORIIA SSSR. UKAZATEL' KNIG I STATEI, VYSHEDSHIKH V 1877-1917 GG. (Moscow, 1957) was intended as a continuation of Mezhov's bibliographies, but unfortunately only the first volume appeared, containing bibliographies of bibliographies now better served by the Glavatskikh work.

For teaching and beginning research the work mentioned above by N.A. Rubakin. SREDI KNIG. Moscow, Nauka, 1913. Volume 2, is also useful.

2.4.2. Soviet period

A major retrospective bibliography of Soviet writings in history is in the process of compilation under the aegis of INION with the cooperation of other major libraries. The project is planned in three volumes, vol. 3 consisting of many parts. The following is the scheme of the bibliography:

Vol. 1-2. Doronin, I.P., et al. ISTORIIA SSSR. UKAZATEL' SOVETSKOI LITERATURY: 1917-1952. Moscow, AN SSSR, 1956-1958. 2 vols in 4.

Vol. 3. ISTORIIA SSSR. UKAZATEL' SOVETSKOI LITERATURY ZA 1917-1967 GG. Tom 3. ISTORIIA SOVETSKOGO OBSHCHESTVA. Moscow, Nauka, 1971-

Vyp. 1. RABOTY PO ISTORII SOVETSKOGO OBSHCHESTVA V TSELOM; not yet published.

Vyp. 2. VELIKAIA OKTIABR'SKAIA SOTSIALISTICHESKAIA REVOLIUTSIIA I GRAZHDANSKAIA VOINA. (MART 1917-1920 GG) of which published was:

Khaskelis, M.L., et al. VELIKAIA OKTIABR'SKAIA SOTSIALISTICHESKAIA REVOLIUTSIIA (MART 1917-MART 1918 GG). UKAZATEL' SOVETSKOI LITERATURY. 1917-1964. Moscow, INION, 12 parts;

Iskol'dskaia, K.K. KUL'TURA I KUL'TURNOE STROITEL'STVO V SOVETSKOI ROSSII. OKTIABR' 1917-1920 GG. UKAZATEL' SOVETSKOI LITERATURY ZA 1917-1967 GG. Moscow, Nauka, 1971. 2 parts.

Vyp. 3. SSSR V PERIOD MIRNOGO SOTSIALISTICHESKOGO STROITEL'STVA. (1921-1941 GG.) not yet published.

Vyp. 4. Kniga 1: Vinogradova, L.B., et al. SSSR V GODY VELIKOI OTECHESTVENNOI VOINY (IIUN' 1941-SENTIABR' 1945 G.). UKAZATEL' SOVETSKOI LITERATURY ZA 1941-1967 GG. Moscow, Nauka, 1977. 2 parts and PRILOZHENIE. SKHEMA KLASSIFIKATSII. VSPOMAGATEL'NYE UKAZATELI.

Kniga 2. Vinogradova, L.B., et al. SSSR V GODY VELIKOI OTECHESTVENNOI VOINY (IIUN' 1941-SENTIABR'1945 G.). GEROI FRONTA I TYLA. UKAZATEL' SOVETSKOI LITERATURY ZA 1941-1967 GG. Moscow, Nauka, 1981.

Soviet work in history other than Russian and Soviet will be covered, when finished, in

Ado, A.V., Meier, M.S., eds. NOVAIA ISTORIIA. UKAZATEL' LITERATURY, IZDANNOI V SSSR NA RUSSKOM IAZYKE. 1917-1940.
Chast' 1. OBSHCHII OTDEL. PERVYI PERIOD NOVOI ISTORII. 1640-1870 GG. Moscow, Universitet, 1980.

From the above discussion it is obvious that much needs to be done to arrive at a reliable, relatively comprehensive, and up - to - date bibliography of both pre-revolutionary and Soviet imprints on Russian history. Historians, therefore, will need to resort to numerous sources such as bibliographies included in monographs (e.g., ISTORIIA SSSR S DREVNEISHIKH VREMEN DO NASHIKH DNEI. Moscow, Nauka, 1966-1980. 12 vols. with bibliographies in each volume), publisher and institutional bibliographies, special(narrow), national, and regional bibliographies, current bibliographies, archival guides, etc. The bibliographies of bibliographies indicated above will help solve part of the problem.

2.5. Indexes to periodicals

The unsatisfactory indexing of general journals, as indicated in Part I, is partly compensated for by the quite extensive search of journals conducted by Mezhov for his bibliographies as well as by the prolific inclusion of literature from journals in Soviet bibliographies. Nevertheless, indexes to journals have considerable bibliographic potential. Masanov's bibliography of indexes (Part I. 4.6.2.3.1.) and G.A. Glavatskikh, ISTORIIA SSSR, will be of special value here.

There are a few recently published indexes which are not registered in the above indicated sources.

They are:

Alatortseva, A.I. ZHURNAL "ISTORIK-MARKSIST". 1926-1941 GG. Moscow, Nauka, 1979.

Schmiegelow-Powell, A. ISTORICHESKIE ZAPISKI. INDEX. VOLUMES 1-90, 1937-1972. Nendeln, Millwood, N.Y., Kraus, 1976.

Schmiegelow-Powell, A. VOPROSY ISTORII. AUTHOR INDEX. 1945-1975. Nendeln, Millwood, N.Y., Kraus, 1977.

Schmiegelow-Powell, A. VOPROSY ISTORII. SUBJECT INDEX. 1945-1975. Nendeln, Millwood, N.Y., Kraus, 1977.

Schmiegelow-Powell, A. ISTORIK-MARKSIST. AUTHOR AND SUBJECT INDEX. 1926-1941. Nendeln, Millwood, N.Y., Kraus, 1981.

2.6. Current bibliographies

Consulting current bibliographies is quite inconvenient because they are either not cumulated at all or cumulation spans only a relatively short period. Therefore, one should consult the various series of the national bibliography, publisher bibliographies, especially the Academy of Sciences annual bibliography and KATALOG KNIG IZDATEL'STVA NAUKA, TRUDY INSTITUTA ISTORII SSSR, bibliography of publications by the Historical Library in Moscow, bibliographies published in historical journals such as VOPROSY ISTORII, VOPROSY DREVNEI ISTORII, SREDNIE VEKA, ISTORIIA KPSS, VOPROSY GERMANSKOI ISTORII, etc. The best tool for carrying out current bibliographic registration is INION's BIBLIOGRAFICHESKII UKAZATEL'. NOVAIA SOVETSKAIA LITERATURA PO OBSHCHESTVENNYM NAUKAM. ISTORIIA, ARKHEOLOGIIA, ETNOGRAFIIA, which has been published monthly since 1947 and has not been cumulated.

2.7. Special bibliographies

Bibliographies of bibliographies will provide access to sources covering historical periods, archeology, chronology, diplomatics, epigraphy, ethnography, geology, heraldry, numismatics, historiography, source study and other subjects. Only historiography, source study, history of science and technology will be discussed below.

2.7.1. Historiography

Historiography is not a bibliographic discipline per se, but it identifies works by and about a given author and works about institutions, schools of thought, etc. Thus it is bibliographic by implication. Major historiographic works are:

Ikonnikov, V.S. OPYT RUSSKOI ISTORIOGRAFII. Kiev, Universitet, 1891-1908. 2 vols.

Rubinstein, N.L. RUSSKAIA ISTORIOGRAFIIA. Moscow, Gospolitizdat, 1941. A textbook.

Shvedova, O.I. ISTORIKI SSSR. UKAZATEL' PECHATNYKH SPISKOV IKH TRUDOV. Moscow, Vsesoiuznaia Knizhnaia Palata, 1941.

Tikhomirov, M.N., ed. OCHERKI ISTORII ISTORICHESKOI NAUKI V SSSR. Moscow, AN SSSR, 1955-1966. 4 vols. (Bibliography is in volume 3.)

The bibliography of historiography is:

Vaisbord, E.A., et al. ISTORIIA ISTORICHESKOI NAUKI V SSSR. DOOKTIABR'SKII PERIOD. BIBLIOGRAFIIA. Moscow, Nauka, 1965.

Eitmontova, R. G., et. al. ISTORIIA ISTORICHESKOI NAUKI V SSSR. SOVETSKII PERIOD. OKTIABR' 1917-1967. BIBLIOGRAFIIA. Moscow, Nauka, 1980. (Volume for Soviet historians in preparation).

See also G.A. Glavatskikh, ISTORIIA SSSR, vol. 1, pp. 109-157.

2.7.2. Source study (arkheografiia, istochnikovedenie)

Historical sources attracted the attention of scholars toward the end of the eighteen century when N.I. Novikov began to publish sources in his DREVNIAIA ROSSIISKAIA VIVLIOFIKA (1773-1775. 10 vols.). Among the earliest critical editions of documents were the PRAVDA RUSSKAIA I SUDEBNIK TSARIA... IVANA VASIL'EVICHA..., prepared by V.N. Tatishchev and published in PRODOLZHENIE DREVNEI

ROSSIISKOI VIVLIOFIKI in 1786. These activities expanded when Rumiantsev sponsored "archeographic" expeditions in search of source materials and subsequently published them. Institutions emerged which concentrated on historic sources, e.g., Obshchestvo istorii i drevnostei rossiiskikh pri Moskovskom universitete (1804), Komissiia pechataniia gosudarstvennykh gramot i dogovorov (1811), Arkheograficheskaia komissiia (1828), Russkoe istoricheskoe obshchestvo (1866). These institutions and societies had their own publications and their bibliographies are of importance. The publications in series can be identified through Masanov's UKAZATELI SODERZHANIIA RUSSKIKH ZHURNALOV. An example of institutional bibliography is:

PODROBNYI KATALOG IZDANII ARKHEOGRAFICHESKOI KOMISSII VYSHEDSHIKH V SVET S 1836 PO 1918 GOD. 6th ed. Petrograd, 1918.

Standard Soviet academic textbooks are:

Tikhomirov, M.N. ISTOCHNIKOVEDENIE ISTORII SSSR. Moscow, OGIZ, 1940. 2 vols. (Vol. 2 prepared S.A. Nikitin).

ISTOCHNIKOVEDENIE ISTORII SSSR. I.D. Koval'chenko, ed. Moscow, Vysshaia shkola, 1981 (previous edition 1973).

ISTOCHNIKOVEDENIE ISTORII SSSR XIX-NACHALA XX V. I.A. Fedosova, et al., eds. Moscow, Universitet, 1970.

Chernomorskii, M.N. ISTOCHNIKOVEDENIE ISTORII SSSR. SOVETSKII PERIOD... Moscow, Vysshaia shkola, 1966.

Literature about published sources in the Soviet Union is listed in

Astrakhantseva, I.F., et al. SOVETSKAIA ARKHEOGRAFIIA. ANNOTIROVANNYI KATALOG NAUCHNO-METODICHESKOI LITERATURY (1917-1970). Moscow, Glavnoe Arkhivnoe Upravlenie 1974. (Vol. 1, no more published).

Annual bibliographies have appeared in ARKHEOGRAFICHESKII EZHEGODNIK since 1957.

A bibliography of the sources themselves can be found in:

Valk, S.N. SOVETSKAIA ARKHEOGRAFIIA. Moscow, AN SSSR, 1948 which lists sources published until 1917 (pp. 120-255) and is continued by

ISTORIIA SOVETSKOI ARKHEOGRAFII. UCHEBNOE POSOBIE. M.S. Seleznev, ed. Moscow, Mosk. gos. istoricheskо-arkhivnyi institut, 1967. 6 vols.

There is also a variety of bibliographies listing special categories of sources, e.g.,: chronicles, memoirs, or travel accounts:

Dmitreva, R.P. BIBLIOGRAFIIA RUSSKOGO LETOPISANIIA. Moscow, AN SSSR, 1962.

Zaionchkovskii, P.A., ed. ISTORIIA DOREVOLIUTSIONNOI ROSSII V DNEVNIKAKH I VOSPOMINANIIAKH. ANNOTIROVANNYI UKAZATEL' KNIG I PUBLIKATSII V ZHURNALAKH. Moscow, Kniga, 1976-

Drobizhev, V.Z., et.al. ISTORIIA SOVETSKOGO OBSHCHESTVA V VOSPOMINANIIAKH SOVREMENNIKOV. ANNOTIROVANNYI UKAZATEL' MEMUARNOI LITERATURY:
v.1. 1917-1957. Moscow, Universitet, 1958;
v.2. pt 1. ZHURNAL'NYE PUBLIKATSII. 1917-1927. Moscow, Kniga, 1961;
pt 2. ZHURNAL'NYE PUBLIKATSII. 1928-1957. Moscow, Kniga, 1967.

Nerhood, H.W. TO RUSSIA AND RETURN. AN ANNOTATED BIBLIOGRAPHY OF TRAVELERS' ENGLISH-LANGUAGE ACCOUNTS OF RUSSIAN FROM THE NINETH CENTURY TO PRESENT. Columbus, OH, Ohio State University Press, 1968.

2.7.3. History of Sciences and Technology

Maichel, K. GUIDE TO RUSSIAN REFERENCE BOOKS. Vol.V. SCIENCE, TECHNOLOGY, AND MEDICINE. Stanford, Hoover Institution, 1967. (HOOVER INSTITUTION BIBLIOGRAPHICAL SERIES, 32).

ISTORIIA ESTESTVOZNANIIA. LITERATURA, OPUBLIKOVANNAIA V SSSR. 1917-1947. Moscow, AN SSSR, 1949- and continuation every five years.

ISTORIIA TEKHNIKI.BIBLIOGRAFICHESKII UKAZATEL'. 1946-1947. Moscow, AN SSSR, 1950- thereafter annually.

The two latter bibliographies are published with an approximate ten years delay.

2.8. Western languages

There are various Western language bibliographies which include, among other things, Russian and Soviet history. These sources are usually very selective. They can be identified through general guides such as Sheehy, op.cit. (See also Part I.)

Bibliographies devoted specifically to Russian history are:

French:

Garnier, E.A. RÉPERTOIRE MÉTHODIQUE DES OUVRAGES EN LANGUE FRANÇAIS RELATIFS À L'EMPIRE DE TOUTES LES RUSSIES QUI SE TROUVENT A LA BIBLIOTHEQUE NATIONALE DE PARIS... HISTOIRE. Paris, E.Rouveyre, 1892. Fasc. 1 by Th. Sabachnikoff, BIBLIOGRAPHIE DE LA RUSSIE.

English:

Crowther, P.A. A BIBLIOGRAPHY OF WORKS IN ENGLISH ON EARLY RUSSIAN HISTORY TO 1800. Oxford, B.H. Blackwell, 1969.

Shapiro, D.M. A SELECT BIBLIOGRAPHY OF WORKS IN ENGLISH ON RUSSIAN HISTORY, 1801-1917. Oxford, B.H. Blackwell, 1962.

East German:

Hellmann, M., ed. OSTEUROPA IN DER HISTORISCHEN FORSCHUNG DER DDR. Dusseldorf, Droste, 1972. 2 vols.

West German:

The Osteuropa-Institut an der Freien Universität Berlin has sponsored several important bibliographies:

Meyer, K. BIBLIOGRAPHIE DER ARBEITEN ZUR OSTEUROPÄISCHEN GESCHICHTE AUS DEN DEUTSCHSPRACHIGEN FACHZEITSCHRIFTEN, 1858-1964. Wiesbaden, O. Harrassowitz, 1966. (BIBLIOGRAPHISCHE MITTELILUNGEN, 9).

Meyer, K. BIBLIOGRAPHIE ZUR OSTEUROPÄISCHEN GESCHICHTE. VERZEICHNIS DER ZWISCHEN 1939 UND 1964 VERÖFFENTLICHTEN LITERATUR IN WESTEUROPÄISCHEN SPRACHEN ZUR OSTEUROPAISCHEN GESCHICHTE BIS 1945. Wiesbaden, O. Harrassowitz, 1972. (BIBLIOGRAPHISCHE MITTELIUNGEN, 10)

and its continuation by

Schmidt, Ch.D. for 1965-1974 published under the same title in 1983 (BIBLIOGRAPHISCHE MITTEILUNGEN, 22).

Späth, M. BIBLIOGRAPHY OF ARTICLES ON EAST-EUROPEAN AND RUSSIAN HISTORY SELECTED FROM ENGLISH LANGUAGE PERIODICALS, 1850-1938. Wiesbaden, O. Harrassowitz, 1981. (BIBLIOGRAPHISCHE MITTEILUNGEN, 20).

2.9. Non-bibliographic reference sources

Historians will take a keen interest in the majority of the sources listed in Part I.5. The field is so overwhelmingly rich that it is impossible here to provide an adequate summary meeting even the most general needs. The reader is advised to resort to such general tools as:

Shapiro, A.L. BIBLIOGRAFIIA ISTORII SSSR... and Zaionchkovskii, P.A. SPRAVOCHNIKI ...

Special areas:

2.9.1. Companion to history

Paxton, J. COMPANION TO RUSSIAN HISTORY. New York, Facts on File, 1983.

2.9.2. Chronology

Alatortseva, A.I., Alekseeva, G.D. 50 LET SOVETSKOI ISTORICHESKOI NAUKI. KHRONIKA NAUCHNOI ZHIZNI. 1917-1967. Moscow, Nauka, 1971.

Kamentseva, E.I. KHRONOLOGIIA. Moscow, Vysshaia shkola, 1967.

2.9.3. Dictionaries

Pushkarev, S.G. DICTIONARY OF RUSSIAN HISTORICAL TERMS FROM THE ELEVENTH CENTURY TO 1917. New Haven, Yale University Press, 1973.

2.9.4. Atlases

Adams, A,E., et al. AN ATLAS OF RUSSIAN AND EAST EUROPEAN HISTORY. New York, Preager, 1967.

Chew, A.F. AN ATLAS OF RUSSIAN HISTORY. New Haven, Yale University Press, 1970.

Drobizhev, V.Z. ISTORICHESKAIA GEOGRAFIIA SSSR. Moscow, Vysshaia shkola, 1973.

Gilbert, M. RUSSIAN HISTORY ATLAS. New York, Macmillan Co., 1972.

RUSSKIE. ISTORIKO-ETNOGRAFICHESKII ATLAS. P.I. Kushnev, ed. Moscow, Nauka, 1967. 2 vols.

2.9.5. Governmental institutions

Amburger, E. GESCHICHTE DER BEHÖRDENORGANIZATION RUSSLANDS VON PETER DEM GROSSEN BIS 1917. Leiden, E.J. Brill, 1966. (STUDIEN ZUR GESCHICHTE OSTEUROPAS, 10).

Eroshkin, N.P. ISTORIIA GOSUDARSTVENNYKH UCHREZHDENII DOREVOLIUTSIONNOI ROSSII. UCHEBNIK... 3rd ed. Moscow, Vysshaia shkola, 1983.

3. Literature

Introduction

The diversity and size of publications in the field of literature present unique bibliographic problems. Literature is published through established publishing houses as well as by individual enterpreneurs and it finds a place in journals of the most diverse types. Literary works and unpublished materials can be found in all humanistically oriented libraries and archives. Literature has ties with all disciplines in the humanities and social sciences. It crosses cultural and national boundaries, and it often appears in formats which elude any categorization as literature. Efforts to organize this vast field has been made by both scholars and bibliographers. Their works are mutually interrelated. Bibliographers will rely on histories of literature and literary criticism while historians of literature will draw on bibliographies. The existing bibliographies do not cover satisfactorily the vast body or "totality" of literary texts, literary history and criticism, theory of literature, literary genres, comparative literatures, and related disciplines. These bibliographies cannot promise easy answers to all research questions, and bibliographic work must be as imaginative as the literature itself.

3.1. Publishing

Printing in Russia remained in the hands of state and Church practically until Catherine II's decree, Ukaz o vol'nykh tipografiiakh, in 1783. Until that time, literary works appeared mainly in manuscript form. The manuscript remained a vehicle for popular literature well into the nineteenth century, and to some extent it still serves certain types of literature, such as the literature of opposition and other literature outside the censorship.

Literature and literary criticism on the printed page in Russia was stimulated by N.I. Novikov's publishing activities, especially through the spread of literary journals promoted by Catherine II and Novikov. A new momentum was introduced by Aleksandr F. Smirdin (publisher after 1829), who paid high royalties for literary works, e.g., to Aleksander S. Pushkin 10 Rb per verse, to Ivan Krylov 40,000 Rb for his BASNE, and a 15,000 Rb annual salary to Senkovskii for editing BIBLIOTEKA DLIA CHTENIIA. He began to print large numbers of copies and sold them at a reasonable price, thus promoting book collecting, readership, and, of course, literature itself. Literature was a standard feature in all major journals. The growth of publishing, now a profitable venture, was tamed only by the high level of illiteracy in Russia. Toward the end of nineteenth century and especially during the first 15 years of the twentieth century the publishing field was rich and diversified. Publishers such as Vol'f, Marks, Sytin and many others produced fine editions of major writers as well as cheap paperbacks. Popular literature has flourished, especially in the twentieth century. Literary criticism has been published in a variety of forms. Again the journals, especially the "tolstye zhurnaly" (thick journals) played a major role in literary and intellectual discussion. Critical reviews and literary supplements were important features. On the other hand, research institutions sponsored and promoted work in literary history and criticism. Among them were: the Academy of Sciences with its committees and sections, e.g., the Arkheograficheskaia kommissiia and Otdelenie russkogo iazyka i slovesnosti; universities; societies of both literary and historical profile, e.g., Obshchestvo liubitelei rossiiskoi slovesnosti pri Moskovskom universitete (1811), Obshchestvo liubitelei drevnei pis'mennosti (St. Petersburg, 1877), Russkoe literaturnoe obshchestvo (St. Petersburg, 1888); and historical societies which were also important for their studies of literature: Obshchestvo istorii i drevnostei rossiiskikh pri Moskovskom universitete (1804), Russkoe istoricheskoe obshchestvo (St. Petersburg, 1866) and others.

For references to these societies see: Zaionchkovskii, op. cit.

From a bibliographic perspective, the scholar must be familiar with all aspects of the publishing industry, the cultural environment in which an author lived and worked, the literary and artistic circles with which he/she associated, the fate of his/her family archives, and the dramatic upheaval of 1917 which affected libraries, archives, and bibliographies in Russia. These and other factors influence the strategy of bibliographic research.

In the Soviet Union the publishing industry has been streamlined. Literature and literary criticism is published by several houses devoted specifically to a special type of literature. The present names of the publishing houses have been used since the reorganization of publishing in 1963. Some of the more important central houses are: Khudozhestvennaia literatura, Sovetskii pisatel', Sovetskaia Rossiia, Sovremennik, Molodaia Gvardiia, Detskaia literatura, and Progress.

Although literary works of importance may be published through any of these houses as well as in republican and regional houses, it will be useful to outline the publishing profiles of the three major ones: Khudozhestvennaia literatura, Sovetskii pisatel', and Nauka.

The Khudozhestvennaia literatura publishing house emerged in 1963 from Gosudarstvennoe izdatel'stvo khudozhestvennoi literatury, formed in 1930 as part of the Ob"edinenie gosudarstvennykh izdatel'stv (OGIZ). Although it stresses Russian literary classics, it publishes Soviet writers as well. Its series are: NARODNAIA BIBLIOTEKA, BIBLIOTEKA SOVETSKOI POEZII, BIBLIOTEKA SOVETSKOI PROZY, BIBLIOTEKA SOVETSKOGO ROMANA, BIBLIOTEKA RUSSKOGO ROMANA, SERIIA LITERATURNYKH MEMUAROV, SOKROVISHCHA LIRICHESKOI POEZII, and others. It publishes journals sponsored by the Soiuz Pisatelei SSSR (Union of Soviet Writers): MOSKVA, NEVA, ZVEZDA. It issues such titles as N(authors's name) V VOSPOMINANIIAKH SOVREMENNIKOV, the collected works of numerous authors, and anthologies. Literature of the Soviet nationalities as well as foreign literature constitute a significant part of its publishing program.

Sovetskii pisatel' is the official publishing house of the Soiuz Pisatelei SSSR. It issues 75 per cent of all new literary works published in the USSR. It was founded in 1938 on the basis of the Moskovskoe tovarishchestvo pisatelei and Izdatel'stvo pisatelei Leningrada. Its major series are: BIBLIOTEKA POETA founded by M. Gorkii in 1931; and DEN' POEZII published annually since 1956 in two issues, one in Moscow and one in Leningrad; MASTERSTVO PEREVODA, and MOLODOI LENINGRAD. Bibliographies such as those compiled by Matsuev (see below), literary criticism, and drama are olso characteristic publications issued by this house. Soiuz Pisatelei SSSR has sponsored several journals. They are issued not through Sovetskii Pisatel', which focuses on books, but through other publishing houses such as Khudozhestvennaia literatura, Pravda, or Izvestiia. Its major journals are: VOPROSY LITERATURY, LITERATURNOE OBOZRENIE, NOVYI MIR, OKTIABR', ZNAMIA, IUNOST', NASH SOVREMENNIK, SOVETSKAIA LITERATURA. Republican Unions of Writers have their own journals.

Khudozhestvennaia literatura and Sovetskii pisatel' have issued bibliographies of their own publications:

KATALOG KNIG IZDATEL'STVA "KHUDOZHESTVENNAIA LITERATURA". 1946-1966. Moscow, Khudozhestvennaia literatura, 1970- and continuation approximately every five years;

Shiperovich, B. IZDATEL'STVO "SOVETSKII PISATEL'". Bibliografiia. 1934-1974. Moscow, Sovetskii Pisatel', 1982.

From a scholarly point of view the most important publisher is the Soviet Academy of Sciences. Its publishing house "Nauka" (its name since 1963) has published complete critical editions of major writers: Lomonosov, Radishchev, Pushkin, Gogol, Lermontov, Turgenev, Lev Tolstoi, Gleb Uspenskii, N.A. Nekrasov, Dostoevskii, Chekhov, Belinskii, Chernyshevskii, Dobroliubov, Gertsen, and Gor'kii. Its quarterly journal is RUSSKAIA LITERATURA. There are several series such as DREVNERUSSKIE LITERATURNYE PAMIATNIKI, LITERATURNOE NASLEDSTVO. The Academy of Sciences sponsors major bibliographies, histories of literature and criticism, and various monographs. Numerous works appear under standardized titles such as N(author's name) V RUSSKOI KRITIKE; N.O LITERATURE; LETOPIS' ZHIZNI I TVORCHESTVA N., N. V IZOBRAZITEL'NOM ISKUSSTVE, N. I EGO SOVREMENNIKI. Information about these publications is available through the Academy of Sciences annual bibliography, the catalog of Nauka publishing house (see Part I. 4.7.), and bibliography of series, e.g., D.V.Oznobishin, LITERATURNYE PAMIATNIKI. SPRAVOCHNIK. Moscow, Nauka, 1984. Information about the Pushkinskii Dom can be found in V.N. Baskakov, PUSHKINSKII DOM. STAT'I. DOKUMENTY, BIBLIOGRAFIIA. Leningrad, Nauka, 1982 and bibliography of its publications for 1905 to 1980 is A.K. Mikhailova, PUSHKINSKII DOM. BIBLIOGRAFIIA TRUDOV. Leningrad, Nauka 1981.

The publishing houses indicated above illustrate only a part of the whole publishing field. Major research institutions, universities, and pedagogical institutes produce a vast amount of materials every year. Furthermore, in the regions and republics local houses publish extensively. There are also research centers, archives, and libraries devoted to a single literary figure, e.g., Tolstoi's museum in Iasnaia Poliana, Turgenev's museum in Orel, Pushkin's museum in Moscow, etc. Unfortunately there is no easy tool which would list and describe them all. General guides, guides in literature, directories of institutions including THE WORLD OF LEARNING, and bibliographies by the institutions themselves and of their publications will offer an indication of the persons associated with them and the work done there. General knowledge of the "structure" of the field will permit an understanding of bibliographic patterns and will facilitate bibliographic research.

3.2. Libraries, Archives, Museums

The most prominent Soviet libraries with holdings in literature are the Saltykov-Shchedrin Public Library in Leningrad, the Pushkinskii Dom Library (also in Leningrad) the Lenin Public Library in Moscow, and regional public libraries. Major private collections donated to libraries quite often are not incorporated in the general holdings but are kept as separate entities. Those which have published catalogs and are of special interest here are:

Smirnov-Sokol'skii, N.P. MOIA BIBLIOTEKA. BIBLIOGRAFICHESKOE OPISANIE. Moscow, Kniga,1969. 2 vols. housed in the Lenin Public Library in Moscow, and

Gol'dberg, V.V. et al., BIBLIOTEKA RUSSKOI POEZII I.N. ROZANOVA. BIBLIOGRAFICHESKOE OPISANIE. Moscow, Kniga, 1975 housed in State A.S. Pushkin's Museum in Moscow.

In the United States the holdings of the Kilgour collection at Harvard are important. There is a published catalog:

Harvard University Library. THE KILGOUR COLLECTION OF RUSSIAN LITERATURE, 1750-1920. Combridge, Mass., Harvard College Library, 1959

and supplement:
Harvard University Library. Houghton Library. THE KILGOUR COLLECTION OF RUSSIAN LITERATURE. Cambridge, Mass., Houghton Library, Harvard University, 1977.

Information about the holdings of other major Western libraries is available through published catalogs.

Literary archival material is scattered in repositories around the world, often in private hands. Guides to archives (Part I. 3.2.4.) will identify major depositories such as the Tsentral'nyi gosudarstvennyi arkhiv literatury i iskusstva in Moscow (founded in 1941) or Rukopisnyi otdel instituta russkoi literatury AN SSSR in Leningrad (founded in 1908). Pre-revolutionary guides to archival materials will have only limited value due to a significant reorganization of Soviet archives, an ongoing process.

A bibliographic search strategy should start with the identification of major repositories,guides to them, and the examination of the guides themselves. It should procede to TEMATIKA ISSLEDOVANII, (see above), and narrow down to monographic literature on a related subject with the hope that archival materials have been identified. However, most of the work in literature requiring archival sources will concentrate on individual authors. Here the LICHNYE ARKHIVNYE FONDY will provide a good start. Resources in the West should also be consulted through library guides.

Literary museums are important depositories of manuscripts, often devoted to one person. The bibliographic technique for locating these materials is the same as for other archival resources.

3.3. Textbooks, guides, bibliographies of bibliographies

The history of bibliography serves as an introduction to its structure and development, and thus it helps to understand the bibliographic network in literary bibliography. In addition to the general history of Russian bibliography (Part I), for the history of literary bibliography see:

Laufer, Iu.M. TEORIIA I METODIKA SOVETSKOI LITERATURNOI BIBLIOGRAFII. ISTORICHESKII OCHERK. Moscow, Kniga, 1978.

Biographies of leading bibliographers will also help e.g.,

Kalent'eva, A.G. VLIUBLENNYI V LITERATURU. OCHERK ZHIZNI I DEIATEL'NOSTI S.A. VENGEROVA, 1855-1920. Moscow, Kniga, 1978.

Vezirova, L.A. I.V. VLADISLAVLEV, 1880-1962. Moscow, Kniga, 1978.

TRIDTSATILETNII IUBILEI LITERATURNOI, BIBLIOGRAFICHESKOI I OBSHCHES'TVENNOI DEIATEL'NOSTI AUGUSTY VLADIMIROVNY MEZ'ER, 1894-1924. BIOGRAFIIA, SPISOK TRUDOV, PRIVETSTVIIA. Leningrad, Kolos, 1926.

Obituaries of bibliographers are useful. These can be found through bibliographies treating book culture (see Part I) or the index to SOVETSKAIA BIBLIOGRAFIIA. Additional sources are the introductions to major bibliographies in this field.

Several guides will introduce students of literature to the structure of the field. An overview of the typology of literary publications, publishing structure, bibliographic methodology, bibliographies, library activities, etc. is provided by:

Bukhshtab, B.Ia., ed. BIBLIOGRAFIIA KHUDOZHESTVENNOI LITERATURY I LITERATUROVEDENIIA. UCHEBNIK DLIA BIBLIOTECHNYKH FAKUL'TETOV INSTITUTOV KUL'TURY. Moscow, Kniga, 1971.

An older guide, and a useful illustration of the ideological changes which affected bibliographic work in literature (when compared with the above) is:

BIBLIOGRAFIIA KHUDOZHESTVENNOI LITERATURY I LITERATUROVEDENIIA. UCHEBNIK DLIA BIBLIOTECHNYKH INSTITUTOV.
Chast' 1. B.Ia. Bukhshtab, ed. Moscow, Sovetskaia Rossiia, 1960;
Chast' 2. E.I. Ryskin, ed. Moscow, Sovetskaia Rossiia, 1958.

Background reading which discusses bibliographic methodology is offered by:

Berkov, P.N. VVEDENIE V TEKHNIKU LITERATUROVEDCHESKOGO ISSLEDOVANIIA. Moscow, Gosuchpedgiz, 1955 and

Gel'fand, N., Libman, V.A., et al. "Potrebnosti nauki i vozmozhnosti bibliografii", VOPROSY LITERATURY 8, 1973: 209-217.

The bibliographic search in literature, like that in other disciplines, should start with bibliographies of bibliographies. Such a source is

Kandel', B.L. RUSSKAIA KHUDOZHESTVENNAIA LITERATURA I LITERATUROVEDENIE. UKAZATEL' SPRAVOCHNO-BIBLIOGRAFICHESKIKH POSOBII S KONTSA XVIII VEKA PO 1974 GOD. Moscow, Kniga, 1976.
rev.: R.N. Krendel', SB 163, 1977:102-105;
N. Gel'fand, VOPROSY LITERATURY 9,1976: 264-268.

and its companion volume for the non-Russian literatures of the Soviet Union:

Erzin, S.A., Ebin, P.E., eds. LITERATURA I FOL'KLOR NARODOV SSSR. UKAZATEL'OTECHESTVENNYKH BIBLIOGRAFICHESKIKH POSOBII I SPRAVOCHNYKH IZDANII, 1926-1970. Moscow, Kniga, 1975.

A still useful guide is the well annotated

Fomin, A.G. PUTEVODITEL' PO BIBLIOGRAFII, BIO-BIBLIOGRAFII, ISTORIOGRAFII, KHRONOLOGII I ENTSIKLOPEDII LITERATURY... 1736-1932 GG. Leningrad, Gosizdat, 1934.

See also for some data supplementary to Kandel':

Ryskin, E.I. BIBLIOGRAFICHESKIE UKAZATELI RUSSKOI LITERATURY XIX V. Moscow, VKP, 1949.

Bibliographies of bibliographies can also be found in general bibliographies of literature. Kandel' can be continued through a search of BIBLIOGRAFIIA SOVETSKOI BIBLIOGRAFII. The source has also introductory surveys which discuss the major bibliographic works published during that year. See also Part I.4.3. for current bibliographies.

3.4. General bibliographies

The number of bibliographies in literature is overwhelming. Since the amount of material published in this field prohibits the preparation of any general comprehensive bibliography, each of them is somewhat limited in scope. An awareness of these limitations is mandatory for users. Furthermore, the scope, the date of publication, sources used for compilation, to some extent even the place of publication, and similar factors will be indicative not only of the limitations of a bibliography but also of changing ideological leanings.

Scholarly bibliographies are available for every period of Russian and Soviet literature. This makes the bibliography in literature different from that in the social sciences, where the pre-revolutionary period is poorly covered as compared with the Soviet era. Nevertheless, the Soviet bibliographies treat the pre-revolutionary literature less thoroughly than Soviet literature . Consequently, the bibliographies published before 1917 such as those by Mezhov, Mez'er, Vengerov, and others retain their value and should not be considered as outdated.

We may delineate the bibliographic network for literature as follows:
Soviet bibliographers have prepared almost comprehensive bibliographies of Soviet imprints dealing with Russian literature up to the seventeenth century. The leading bibliographies are:

Droblenkova, N.F. BIBLIOGRAFIIA SOVETSKIKH RUSSKIKH RABOT PO LITERATURE XI-XVII VV. ZA 1917-1957 GG. Moscow-Leningrad, AN SSSR, 1961.

Droblenkova, N.F. BIBLIOGRAFIIA RABOT PO DREVNE-RUSSKOI LITERATURE, OPUBLIKOVANNYKH V SSSR 1958-1967 GG.
Chast' 1. 1958-1962 GG. Leningrad, Nauka, 1978;
Chast' 2. 1963-1967 GG. Leningrad, Nauka, 1979.

In addition there are specialized bibliographies which encompass both Russian and Soviet imprints. Examples of these are:

Dmitreva, R.P. BIBLIOGRAFIIA RUSSKOGO LETOPISANIIA. Moscow-Leningrad, AN SSSR, 1962.

Peretts, V.P. DREVNERUSSKAIA POVEST'. Moscow-Leningrad, AN SSSR, 1940. (BIBLIOGRAFIIA DREVNE-RUSSKOI LITERATURY, 1).

Nazarevskii, A.A. BIBLIOGRAFIIA DREVNERUSSKOI POVESTI. Moscow-Leningrad, AN SSSR, 1955.

Still the Soviet bibliographers left significant gaps in covering the pre-1917 imprints. For those scholars are referred to:

Mez'er, A.V. RUSSKAIA SLOVESNOST' S XI PO XIX STO-LETIE VKLIUCHITEL'NO. BIBLIOGRAFICHESKII UKA-ZATEL' PROIZVEDENII RUSSKOI SLOVESNOSTI V SVIAZI

S ISTORIEI LITERATURY I KRITIKI. KNIGI I ZHURNAL'NYIA STAT'I. St. Petersburg, Tip. Porokhovshchikova, 1899-1902. 2 vols.
rev.: D.N. Abramovich, IZVESTIIA OTDELENIIA RUSSKOGO IAZYKA I SLOVESNOSTI, 1901;
A.P. Al'bitskii, "Novyi trud po bibliografii...", LITERATURNYI VESTNIK I,1903:80-87;
RUSSKOE BOGATSTVO 1,1900:99-102.

For the eighteenth century and up to 1917 Soviets have published major general bibliographies covering both Russian and Soviet imprints with an obvious emphasis on the Soviet publications, so that the Mez'er bibliography also retains to a great extent its value for this period. The bibliographies listed below constitute a fundamental resource for any work in Russian literature and familiarity with them is mandatory for all its students. The prefaces and reviews delineate such important factors as sources of compilation, comprehensiveness, editorial principles, and permit their scholarly standards to be judged.

Stepanov, V.P., Stennik, Iu.V. ISTORIIA RUSSKOI LITERATURY XVIII V. BIBLIOGRAFICHESKII UKAZATEL'. Leningrad, Nauka, 1968.
rev.:I.F. Martynov, SB 112, 1968:58-63.

Muratova, K.D. ed. ISTORIIA RUSSKOI LITERATURY XIX VEKA. BIBLIOGRAFICHESKII UKAZATEL'. Moscow-Leningrad, AN SSSR, 1962.
rev.:B. Ia. Bukhshtab, SB 86, 1964:79-88;
R.N. Krendel', VESTNIK AN SSSR 3, 1963:143-144;
S.V. Belov, VOPROSY LITERATURY 1,1968:232-233.

Muratova, K.D., ed. ISTORIIA RUSSKOI LITERATURY KONTSA XIX- NACHALA XX VEKA. BIBLIOGRAFICHESKII UKAZATEL'. Moscow-Leningrad, AN SSSR, 1963.
rev.:B.Ia. Bukhshtab, SB 86, 1964:79-88;
N. Gel'fand, VOPROSY LITERATURY 5, 1964:227-229;
N.I. Matsuev, NOVYI MIR 40, 1964:258-260.

Several sources complement the above

bibliographies and Kandel', RUSSKAIA KHUDOZHESTVENNAIA LITERATURA... offers a satisfactory guide to them.

A different category and tradition is represented by several monumental, although unfinished works by S.A. Vengerov:

ISTOCHNIKI SLOVARIA RUSSKIKH PISATELEI. St. Petersburg, Akademiia Nauk, 1900-1917. 4 vols. (A to Nekrasov).

KRITIKO-BIOGRAFICHESKII SLOVAR' RUSSKIKH PISATELEI. St. Petersburg, 1889-1904. 6 vols. (A to Bogoiavlenskii), and its shorter version

KRITIKO-BIOGRAFICHESKII SLOVAR' RUSSKIKH PISATELEI Petrograd, 1915-1918. 2 vols. (A-Pavlov).

Practical bibliographies providing a good starting point for bibliographic research are:

Rubakin, N. SREDI KNIG, vol. 1...
and Wytrzens, G., see below.

Soviet literature does not have a comprehensive retrospective bibliography. Quite exhaustive coverage is provided by current bibliographies published in parts and not cumulated. Literary criticism, however, is well captured by Ryskin (below) for the period 1917-1962.

Retrospective bibliographies by and about writers are:

RUSSKIE SOVETSKIE PISATELI. PROZAIKI. BIBLIOGRAFICHESKII UKAZATEL'. Leningrad, [SS], (from vol. 4 Moscow, Kniga), 1959-1972. 7 vols.

RUSSKIE SOVETSKIE PISATELI. POETY. BIBLIOGRAFICHESKII UKAZATEL'. Moscow, Kniga, 1977-

For poetry consulted should be:

Tarasenkov, A. RUSSKIE POETY XX VEKA. 1900-1956. BIBLIOGRAFIIA. Moscow, Sovetskii pisatel', 1966.

For earlier Soviet period still valuable are:

Vitman, A.M., et al. VOSEM' LET RUSSKOI KHUDOZHESTVENNOI LITERATURY (1917-1925). BIBILIOGRAFICHESKII SPRAVOCHNIK. Moscow-Leningrad, Gosizdat, 1929.

Vladislavlev, I.V. LITERATURA VELIKOGO DESIATILETIIA, 1917-1927. Moscow-Leningrad, Gosizdat, 1928.

An excellent place to start a bibliographic search in Russian literature for all periods, for teaching and research purposes, for literary works and criticism as well as for reference materials are the bibliographies prepared by G. Wytrzens, published by V. Klostermann in Frankfurt am Main as SONDERHEFT in the series ZEITSCHRIFT FÜR BIBLIOTHEKSWESEN UND BIBLIOGRAPHIE (ZBB):

BIBLIOGRAPHISCHE EINFÜHRUNG IN DAS STUDIUM DER SLAVISCHEN LITERATUREN. 1972 (ZBB, 13).

BIBLIOGRAPHIE DER LITERATURWISSENSCHAFTLICHEN SLAWISTIK, 1970-1980. 1982 (ZBB, 36).

BIBLIOGRAPHIE DER RUSSISCHEN AUTOREN UND ANONYMEN WERKE. 1975 (ZBB, 19).

BIBLIOGRAPHIE DER RUSSISCHEN AUTOREN UND ANONYMEN WERKE, 1975-1980. 1982 (ZBB, 37).

3.5. Indexes to periodicals, serials, literary almanacs, collections of papers

Bibliographic work in literature is complicated by the fact that numerous important contributions are published in various serials and collections of works. Since comprehensive bibliographic works do not exist there will be an almost inevitable necessity of expanding the bibliographic search beyond existing bibliographies into serials and collections. Indexes to serials can be identified through Iu.I. Masanov's bibliography of indexes, op.cit. Among the indexes not covered by Masanov are:

NEW CONTENTS. SLAVISTICS. INHALTSVERZEICHNISSE SLAVISTISCHER ZEITSCHRIFTEN. CONTENTS OF CURRENT

PERIODICALS IN THE FIELD OF SLAVIC LINGUISTICS, LITERATURE, AND FOLKLORE. Bayerische Staatsbibliothek, ed. Munchen, O. Sagner, 1976- quarterly.

Miller, T.N. BIBLIOGRAPHICAL INDEX TO THE CONTRIBUTIONS TO NOVYI MIR, 1925-1934. Ann Arbor, Mich., Ardis, 1983.

Kleimenova, R.N. SISTEMATICHESKAIA ROSPIS' IZDANII OBSHCHESTVA LIUBITELEI ROSSIISKOI SLOVESNOSTI PRI MOSKOVSKOM UNIVERSITETE. 1811-1930. Moscow, Universitet, 1981.

Franz, E. AKADEMIIA NAUK SSSR. OTDELENIE RUSSKOGO IAZYKA I SLOVESNOSTI. SBORNIK. UKAZATEL' SODERZHANIIA K TOMAM 1-101 (1867-1926/28). Nendeln, Kraus, 1978.

Stepanov, V.P. ZHURNAL "RUSSKAIA LITERATURA" ZA 1958-1973 GG. UKAZATEL' SODERZHANIIA. Leningrad, Nauka, 1975.

Collections of literary works and criticism which cannot be characterized either as monographs or series, called in Russian almanakh and sbornik (in English miscellany), have their own bibliographies:

Smirnov-Sokol'skii, N.P. RUSSKIE LITERATURNYE AL'MANAKHI I SBORNIKI XVIII-XIX V. Moscow, Kniga, 1965.

LITERATURNO-KHUDOZHESTVENNYE AL'MANAKHI I SBORNIKI. BIBLIOGRAFICHESKII UKAZATEL'. Moscow, VKP:
Vol. 1: 1900-1911. O.D. Golubeva, comp., 1957;
Vol. 2: 1912-1917. N.P. Rogozhin, comp., 1958;
Vol. 3: 1918-1927. N.P. Rogozhin, comp., 1960;
Vol. 4: 1928-1937. O.D. Golubeva, comp., 1959.

After 1937 this category of publication is covered in the bibliographies prepared by N.I. Matsuev cited below.

3.6. Current bibliographies.

Nikolai I. Matsuev (1894-1975) attempted to conduct current comprehensive registration of literary publications. There are differences in comprehensiveness and arrangement between the various volumes of his bibliography of which users should be aware. The introductions to each volume should be consulted before using Matsuev's bibliographies. There were different series published:

1. Matsuev, N.I. KHUDOZHESTVENNAIA LITERATURA RUSSKAIA I PEREVODNAIA:
   1917-1925. UKAZATEL' STATEI I RETSENZII. Moscow-Odessa, Izd-vo knizhno-bibliotechnykh rabotnikov, 1926;
   1926-1928. BIBLIOGRAFICHESKII UKAZATEL'. Moscow, Izd-vo knizhno-bibliotechnykh rabotnikov, 1929;
   1929-1932. UKAZATEL' STATEI, RETSENZII I ANNOTATSII. Moscow, Goslitizdat, 1936;
   1933-1937. V OTSENKE KRITIKI. 1933-1937. BIBLIOGRAFICHESKII UKAZATEL'. Moscow, Goslitizdat, 1940;

2. KHUDOZHESTVENNAIA LITERATURA RUSSKAIA I PEREVODNAIA. 1938-1953 GG. BIBLIOGRAFIIA. Moscow, Goslitizdat,1956-1959.
   2 vols: Vol. 1 for 1938-1945. 1956;
   Vol. 2 for 1946-1953. 1959.

3. Matusev, N.M. SOVETSKAIA KHUDOZHESTVENNAIA LITERATURA I KRITIKA. BIBLIOGRAFIIA. 1938-1948. Moscow, Sovetskii Pisatel', 1952- and continuation approximately every two years. Last issue published was 1964-1965 in 1972.

The content of these bibliographies compares with each other as follows:

Ad 1. contains Russian pre-revolutionary, Soviet, and foreign authors in Russian translation, all followed by Russian criticism. Since 1933 also folklore and literary criticism published in book form.

Ad 2. covers world literature and Russian pre-revolutionary literature, works by pre-revolutionary critics, and Soviet criticism on non-

Soviet literatures, i.e., literature and criticism not covered by SOVETSKAIA KHUDOZHESTVENNAIA LITERATURA for the overlapping years.
Ad 3. has works by and about Soviet writers and Soviet criticism if published in book form and reviewed, i.e., by and about Soviet critics. Beginning with 1952-1953 literary criticism published in journals has also been included.

Literary theory, history and criticism not covered by Matsuev can be found in a bibliography which began as a retrospective work and is now published continously in three-year intervals with a delay of about five years:

Ryskin, Iu.D. SOVETSKOE LITERATUROVEDENIE I KRITIKA. RUSSKAIA SOVETSKAIA LITERATURA. 1917-1962. Moscow, Nauka, 1966;
1963-1967. Moscow, Nauka, 1970;
and continuation.
In vol. for 1968-1970 published in 1975 Ryskin introduced section "Personalia" which continues Matsuev bibliographies. Exception are years 1966-1967.

Currently continuing bibliography can be found in:

BIBLIOGRAFICHESKII UKAZATEL'. NOVAIA SOVETSKAIA LITERATURA PO OBSHCHESTVENNYM NAUKAM. LITERATUROVEDENIE. Moscow, INION, 1947- monthly.

Modern Language Association of America. INTERNATIONAL BIBLIOGRAPHY. New York, 1921-
This source recently increased the inclusion of Slavic titles and can be searched on-line.

Prolific bibliographic activities are carried on by regional and republican libraries (see Part I.4.5.). Their current bibliographies (often with the generic title BIBLIOGRAFIIA O... OBLASTI) are important for literary works and criticism. Furthermore, bio-bibliographic dictionaries (also with more or less standardized titles such as PISATELI IUZHNOGO URALA) combine data by and about literary writers.

In conclusion:

Suggestions for a retrospective bibliographic search of Russian literature:

Basic bibliographic search:
Wytrzens.

Advanced general bibliographic search:
Prior to the eighteenth century: Mez'er followed by Droblenkova for the Soviet period;
Eighteen century: Mez'er followed by Stepanov (to 1966);
Nineteenth century: Mez'er followed by Muratova (to 1959);
1900-1917: Muratova (to 1962);
Soviet literature: RUSSKIE SOVETSKIE PISATELI. PROZAIKI and POETY which cumulate almost entirely Matsuev;
Soviet criticism: Ryskin who expands Matsuev by theory and history of literature and since 1968 continues his "Personalia".

3.7. Russian literature and criticism in Western languages

There are two bibliographic components in this category: translations from the Russian (mainly belles lettres themselves) and criticism of Russian literature originally written in Western languages. Since the Soviet bibliographies do not cover these adequately (especially the latter category) and the Western bibliographies distinguish between them, the bibliographic search strategy will have to be organized accordingly.

In general, of course, materials published in the West are registered in such sources as: CUMULATIVE BOOK INDEX, INDEX TRANSLATIONUM, national bibliographies, bibliographies of Slavic and East European studies in general, the MLA bibliography, and the like. These sources can be identified through Sheehy, op. cit. Publications issued in the Soviet Union in Western languages are listed in the Soviet national bibliography in the series KNIZHNAIA LETOPIS' and EZHEGODNIK KNIGI, both offering adequate indexes to these materials.

For translations see:

Lewański, R.C. THE LITERATURE OF THE WORLD IN ENGLISH TRANSLATION. A BIBLIOGRAPHY. Vol. II. THE SLAVIC LITERATURES. New York, The New York Public Library and F. Ungar, 1971.

PROIZVEDENIIA SOVETSKIKH PISATELEI V PEREVODAKH NA INOSTRANNYE IAZYKI. OTDEL'NYE ZARUBEZHNYE IZDANIIA. BIBLIOGRAFICHESKII UKAZATEL'. Moscow, Soiuz Pisatelei SSSR, 1954- (with coverage beginning 1945-).

For text and criticism see:

Line, M.B. BIBLIOGRAPHY OF RUSSIAN LITERATURE IN ENGLISH TRANSLATION TO 1900. (EXCLUDING PERIODICALS). London, Library Association, 1963.

Ettinger, A., Gladstone, J.M. RUSSIAN LITERATURE, THEATRE, AND ART. A BIBLIOGRAPHY OF WORKS IN ENGLISH, PUBLISHED 1900-1945. Port Washington, N.Y., Kennikat Press, 1971.

Gibian, G. SOVIET RUSSIAN LITERAURE IN ENGLISH. A CHECKLIST BIBLIOGRAPHY... Ithaca, N.Y., Center for International Studies, Cornell University, 1967.

Law, A.H., Goslett, P.C. SOVIET PLAYS IN TRANSLATION. AN ANNOTATED BIBLIOGRAPHY. New York, CASTA, 1981.

Bamborschke, U., Werner, W. BIBLIOGRAPHIE SLAVISTISCHER ARBEITEN AUS DEN WICHTIGSTEN ENGLISCHSPRACHIGEN FACHZEITSCHRIFTEN, SOWIE FEST- UND SAMMELSCHRIFTEN, 1922-1976. Wiesbaden, O. Harrassowitz, 1981. (BIBLIOGRAPHISCHE MITTEILUNGEN, 19).

Terry, G.M. EAST EUROPEAN LANGUAGES AND LITERATURES. A SUBJECT AND NAME INDEX TO ARTICLES IN ENGLISH-LANGUAGE JOURNALS, 1900-1977. Oxford, Clio Press, 1978.

Terry, G.M. EAST EUROPEAN LANGUAGES AND LITERATURES. 2. A SUBJECT AND NAME INDEX TO ARTICLES IN FESTSCHRIFTEN, CONFERENCE PROCEEDINGS, AND COLLECTED PAPERS IN THE ENGLISH LANGUAGE, 1900-1981, INCLUDING ARTICLES IN JOURNALS, 1978-1981. Nottingham, Astra Press, 1982.

Seemann, K.D. BIBLIOGRAPHIE SLAVISTISCHEN ARBEITEN AUS DEN DEUTSCHSPRACHIGEN FACHZEITSCHRIFTEN. 1876-1963. Wiesbaden, O. Harrassowitz, 1965. (BIBLIOGRAPHISCHE MITTEILUNGEN, 8).

Bamborschke, U., et al. BIBLIOGRAPHIE SLAVISTISCHER ARBEITEN AUS DEUTSCHSPRACHIGEN FACHZEITSCHRIFTEN, 1964-1973: EINSCHLIESSLICH SLAVISTISCHER ARBEITEN AUS DEUTSCHPRACHIGEN NICHTSLAVISTISCHEN ZEITSCHRIFTEN SOWIE SLAVISTISCHEN FEST- UND SAMMELSCHRIFTEN, 1945-1973. Wiesbaden, O. Harrassowitz, 1976. 2 vols. (BIBLIOGRAPHISCHE MITTEILUNGEN, 13).

Kaiser, E., Hansak, E. MATERIALIEN ZU EINER SLAVISTICHEN BIBLIOGRAPHIE. ARBEITEN DER IN DER BUNDESREPUBLIK DEUTSCHLAND, ÖSTERREICH UND DER DEUTSCHSPRACHIGEN SCHWEIZ TÄTIGEN SLAVISTEN. 1973-1983. Munchen, O. Sagner, 1983.

Work on Russian literature is conducted world wide and both national bibliographies as well as specialized bibliographies published in various countries will reflect it. Scholars should refer to Sheehy, op. cit. and to bibliographies of bibliographies in the countries of their interest.

We cannot provide adequate coverage of translations from foreign languages into Russian, an area which sometimes is of importance to students of Russian literature. The main repository of foreign literature in the Soviet Union is the Library of Foreign Literature in Moscow, which enjoys national library status. Consequently information on its activities is of interest. This is provided in IZDANIIA VGBIL. VYBOROCHNYI BIBLIOGRAFICHESKII UKAZATEL'. 1941-1981. Moscow, 1982. Translations into Russian are scattered in numerous sources. Again convenient places to begin a search are the Soviet national bibliography, Matsuev's bibliographies, op. cit., and IZDANIIA VGBIL, op.cit. Some authors or literatures will have their own bibliographies. Bibliographies of a single author are frequently prepared by the VGBIL. For American scholars particularly interesting is:

Libman, V.A. AMERIKANSKAIA LITERATURA V RUSSKIKH PEREVODAKH I KRITIKE. BIBLIOGRAFIIA, 1776-1975. Moscow, Nauka, 1977. (An earlier edition is outdated).

3.8. Émigré literature.

Soviet bibliographies do not list emigre literature. Western efforts to register it are also modest. Consequently, in addition to bibliographies, histories of Russian emigre literatures and anthologies will be useful. In the latter category the most recent work is:

Pachmuss T. A RUSSIAN CULTURAL REVIVAL; A CRITICAL ANTHOLOGY OF EMIGRE LITERATURE BEFORE 1939. Knoxville, The University of Tennessee Press, 1981.

Western bibliographies of Russian literature such as Wytrzens, op. cit., AMERICAN BIBLIOGRAPHY OF SLAVIC AND EAST EUROPEAN STUDIES, etc. will often include emigre literature.

Bibliographies devoted directly to Russian emigre literature are:

Foster, L. BIBLIOGRAPHY OF RUSSIAN ÉMIGRÉ LITERATURE, 1918-1968. Boston, G.K. Hall, 1970. 2 vols.

Shtein, E. POEZIIA RUSSKOGO RASSEIANIIA, 1920-1977. Ashford, Conn., Lad'iam, 1978.

Woll, J. SOVIET DISSIDENT LITERATURE. A CRITICAL GUIDE. Boston, G.K. Hall, 1983.

See also Part I.4.9.

3.9. Special Bibliographies

The wealth of subject bibliographies in literature can be approached through bibliographies of bibliographies and especially B. Kandel', op. cit. Area studies such as textology, folklore and comparative literature merit somewhat greater attention. For drama see theater, Part II. 5.2.2.

3.9.1. Textology

Naidich, E.E. OT KANTEMIRA DO CHEKHOVA. OSNOVNYE SOVETSKIE IZDANIIA SOCHINENII RUSSKIKH PISATELEI XVIII-NACHALA XX V. SPRAVOCHNOE POSOBIE. Moscow, Kniga, 1984.

Zheltova, N.I., Kolesnikova, M.I. TVORCHESKAIA ISTORIIA PROIZVEDENII RUSSKIKH I SOVETSKIKH PISATELEI. BIBLIOGRAFICHESKII UKAZATEL'. Moscow, Kniga, 1968.

Lebedeva, E.D. TEKSTOLOGIIA: VOPROSY TEORII. UKAZATEL' SOVETSKIKH RABOT ZA 1917-1981 GG. Moscow, INION, 1982, continues her

TEKSTOLOGIIA RUSSKOI LITERATURY XVIII-XX VV. UKAZATEL' SOVETSKIKH RABOT NA RUSSKOM IAZYKE, 1917-1975 GG. Moscow, INION, 1978.

Lebedeva, E.D. TEKSTOLOGIIA: TRUDY MEZHDUNARODNOI EDITSIONNO-TEKSTOLOGICHESKOI KOMISSII PRI MEZHDUNARODNOM KOMITETE SLAVISTOV. UKAZATEL' DOKLADOV I PUBLIKATSII, 1958-1978. Moscow, INION, 1980.

3.9.2. Folklore

The leading journal RUSSKII FOL'KLOR contains numerous subject bibliographies. Folkore is often registered in literary bibliographies. Retrospective and current bibliographic work is conducted by:

Mel'ts, M.Ia. RUSSKII FOL'KLOR. BIBLIOGRAFICHESKII UKAZATEL'. 3 vols: 1917-1944, 1945-1959, 1960-1965; Leningrad, Nauka, 1961-1967. The volume for 1900-1916 was published in Leningrad, Biblioteka Akademii Nauk SSSR, 1981.

3.9.3. Comparative literature

See N.P. Bannikova, V.A. Libman, J.S.G. Simmons,

all op.cit.

3.10. Non-bibliographic reference sources

Literature is particularly rich in non-bibliographic reference sources such as: encyclopedias, bibliographic dictionaries, chronicles of cultural events, dictionaries of pseudonyms, quotations. (See Part I). Sources dealing with dictionaries of a single author's language, chronologies, dictionaries of an author's acquaintances, pictorial representations, etc. can be identified through bibliographies dealing with the individual author, which in turn are listed in bibliographies of bibliographies, guides and other general reference sources.

4. Russian linguistics and language studies

4.1. Institutions

Language studies have been and still are concentrated around a few major centers. Outside Russia there were the Universities in Vienna, Prague, Belgrade, and Warsaw. The latter moved to Rostov-on-Don in 1915. In Russia Novorossiiskii Universitet in Odessa, universities in Kazan, Dorpat (now Tartu) and, of course, Moscow, St.Petersburg and the Academy of Sciences were most prominent. Most of the work of these and other centers was published in their series and journals: UCHENYE ZAPISKI, IZVESTIIA, SBORNIK, OTCHETY, as well as in specialized journals such as ARCHIV FÜR SLAVISCHE PHILOLOGIE, ZEITSCHRIFT FÜR SLAVISCHE PHILOLOGIE, RUSSKII FILOLOGICHESKII VESTNIK, FILOLOGICHESKIE ZAPISKI.

Since the Revolution the Institut russkogo iazyka at the Academy of Sciences of the USSR has played the leading research and publishing role in Russian language studies. Its publications are registered not only in the bibliographies of langauge and philology but also in the Academy of Sciences' own annual bibliography. The leading publisher in this field besides Nauka is Russkii iazyk, established in 1974. Almost all institutions of higher learning which stress humanistic studies publish their research in a variety of collections, works, proceedings, etc., since monographs in this discipline are not issued in abundance.

Important archival sources for the study of Russian language are housed in the Academy of Sciences. Information on holdings is provided by

Kotkov, S.I., Sumkina, A.I. LINGVISTICHESKIE ISTOCHNIKI, FONDY INSTITUTA RUSSKOGO IAZYKA. Moscow, Nauka, 1967. (Information about this and other SBORNIKI published by this Institut can be found in S.I. Kotkov, ed., ISTOCHNIKI PO ISTORII RUSSKOGO IAZYKA. Moscow, Nauka, 1976. 249-264).

4.2. History of language studies

Histories of language studies can be bibliographically valuable. Among the most useful are:

Jagić, I.V. ISTORIIA SLAVIANSKOI FILOLOGII. St.Petersburg, Akademiia Nauk, 1910 (ENTSIKLOPEDIIA SLAVIANSKOI FILOLOGII, vyp.1).

Bulich, S.K. OCHERK ISTORII IAZYKOZNANIIA V ROSSII. St. Petersburg, 1904 (ZAPISKI ISTORIKO-FILOLOGICHESKOGO FAKUL'TETA IMP. SANKTPETERBURGSKAGO UNIVERSITETA, T. 75).

Berezin, F.M. OCHERKI PO ISTORII IAZYKOZNANIIA V ROSSII: KONETS 19-NACHALO 20 VEKA. Moscow, Nauka, 1968.

Amirova, T.A. OCHERKI PO ISTORII LINGVISTIKI. Moscow, Glav. red. Vostochnoi literatury, 1975.

SOVETSKOE IAZYKOZNANIE ZA 50 LET (1917-1967). Moscow, Nauka, 1967.

See also the encyclopedia:

RUSSKII IAZYK. ENTSIKLOPEDIIA. Moscow, Russkii iazyk, 1980.

4.3. Bibliographies of bibliographies

Almost all the guides and bibliographies of bibliographies discussed in Part I have chapters dealing with language studies. Specialized bibliographies of bibliographies in linguisties are:

Kukushkina, E.S., Stepanova, A.G. BIBLIOGRAFIIA BIBLIOGRAFII PO IAZYKOZNANIIU. ANNOTIROVANNYI SISTEMATICHESKII UKAZATEL' OTECHESTVENNYKH IZDANII. Moscow, [MPB], 1963.

Schaller, H.W. BIBLIOGRAPHIE DER BIBLIOGRAPHIEN ZUR SLAVISCHEN SPRACHWISSENSCHAFT. Frankfurt am Main, Lang, 1982. (Symbolae Slavicae, 15).

4.4. General linguistics and language studies

Debets, N.P., et al. BIBLIOGRAFICHESKII UKAZATEL' LITERATURY PO IAZYKOZNANIIU, IZDANNOI V SSSR S 1918 PO 1957 G. Moscow, 1958;
Vyp. 1. KNIGI I SBORNIKI NA RUSSKOM IAZYKE, IZDANNYE V SSSR 1918-1955. Moscow, AN SSSR, 1958 is the only volume published out of 5 volumes planned.

Although largely replaced by subsequent bibliographies, it is still a handy tool for identifing dissertations, conferences, bibliographies, histories not only in Slavic, but also in other languages. It lists only monographs.

Ashnin, F.D., et al. OBSHCHEE IAZYKOZNANIE. BIBLIOGRAFICHESKII UKAZATEL' LITERATURY, IZDANNOI V SSSR S 1918 PO 1962 G. Moscow, Nauka, 1965.

Ashnin, F.D., et al. STRUKTURNOE I PRIKLADNOE IAZYKOZNANIE. BIBLIOGRAFICHESKII UKAZATEL' LITERATURY, IZDANNOI V SSSR S 1918 PO 1962 G. Moscow, Nauka, 1965.

These titles are continued by:

Malinskaia, B.A., Ghabat, M.Ts. OBSHCHEE I PRIKLADNOE IAZYKOZNANIE. UKAZATEL' LITERATURY, IZDANNOI V SSSR S 1963 PO 1967 G. Moscow, Nauka, 1972; for 1968-1977. Moscow, INION, 1981- in 13 vols (each devoted to a different subject);

Malinskaia, B.A., et al. ONOMASTIKA. UKAZATEL' LITERATURY, IZDANNOI V SSSR S 1963 PO 1970 G. Moscow, INION, 1976 and a continuation for 1971-1975 with a supplement for 1918-1962 published in 1978. Last issue 1967-1980 was published in 1984.

A special focus has

Zinin, S.I. ANTROPONOMIKA. BIBLIOGRAFICHESKII UKAZATEL' LITERATURY NA RUSSKOM IAZYKE. Tashkent, 1968.

4.5. Slavic (including Russian) language studies

This category is the most useful type of bibliography for Russian linguisits, since bibliographies devoted exclusively to the Russian language are few and already quite out of date (below). Registration of current publications in Slavic linguisitics began quite early. The pioneering work was done by:

Akademiia Nauk SSSR. Otdelenie russkogo iazyka i slovesnosti. IZVESTIIA 1901- (bibliographic coverage for 1900).

This was continued by:

ROCZNIK SLAWISTYCZNY. REVUE SLAVISTIQUE. Warszawa, 1908- (except for the years 1918-1928 it is still an ongoing annual service, unfortunately with significant delay).

Faster, although more selective, is the annual:

Modern Language Association. INTERNATIONAL BIBLIOGRAPHY OF BOOKS AND ARTICLES ON THE MODERN LANGUAGES AND LITERATURES. New York, 1957- (recently more inclusive for Slavic languages).

The best tools to trace current publications are INION's

BIBLIOGRAFICHESKII UKAZATEL':

NOVAIA SOVETSKAIA LITERATURA PO OBSHCHESTVENNYM NAUKAM. IAZYKOZNANIE;

NOVAIA INOSTRANNAIA LITERATURA PO OBSHCHESTVENNYM NAUKAM. IAZYKOZNANIE.
Both monthlies, not cumulated (since 1954-).

The best registration of Soviet works is provided by:

Debets, N.P., et al. SLAVIANSKOE IAZYKOZNANIE. BIBLIOGRAFICHESKII UKAZATEL' LITERATURY, IZDANNOI V SSSR S 1918 PO 1960 GG. Moscow, AN SSSR, 1963: Part 1: 1918-1955;

Part 2: 1956-1960,
and continuations for the years:
1961-1965, published in 1969.
1966-1970, published in 1973.

Beginning with the volume for 1971-1975 the bibliography is published in two parallel parts:

ISTORIIA SLAVIANSKOGO IAZYKOZNANIIA. RUSSKII IAZYK, (published in 1980) and SLAVIANSKIE IAZYKI. PRIKLADNOE IAZYKOZNANIE, (published in 1981).

Bibliographic search can be expanded through:

Girke, W., et. al. HANDBIBLIOGRAPHIE ZUR NEUEREN LINGUISTIK IN OSTEUROPA. 1963-1965. München, W. Fink, 1974 continued as
Band II: HANDBIBLIOGRAPHIE ZUR SLAVISTISCHEN UND ALLGEMEINEN LINGUISTIK IN OSTEUROPA. 1966-1971. Tübingen, M. Niemeyer, 1980.
Band III for 1972-1977 is in preparation.

Stankiewicz, E., Worth, D.S. A SELECTED BIBLIOGRAPHY OF SLAVIC LINGUISTICS. The Hague, Mouton, 1966-1970. 2 vols. (SLAVISTICS PRINTINGS AND REPRINTINGS, XLIX, 1 AND 2).

Koschmieder, E., Schaller, H.W. BIBLIOGRAPHIE ZUR SLAVISCHEN SPRACHWISSENSCHAFT. Frankfurt am Main; Lang, 1977. (Symbolae Slavicae, 1).

Special bibliographies:

Brang, P., Züllig, M. KOMMENTIERTE BIBLIOGRAPHIE ZUR SLAVISCHEN SOZIOLINGUISTIK. Bern, Peter Lang, 1981. 3 vols. (Slavica Helvetica, 17).

Korotkina, B.M. MEZHDUNARODNYE KONGRESSY PO IAZYKOZNANIIU. BIBLIOGRAFICHESKIII UKAZATEL' [v 3-kh ch] vyp. 2. SLAVIANSKIE IAZYKI. Leningrad, BAN, 1983, a sequel to the edition of 1973.

4.6. Russian language

In addition to bibliographies dealing with Slavic languages (4.5), there are two important retrospective bibliographies:

Avilova, N.S., et. al. BIBLIOGRAFICHESKII UKAZATEL' LITERATURY PO RUSSKOMU IAZYKOZNANIIU S 1825 PO 1880 G. Moscow, AN SSSR, 1954-1959. 8 vols.

Unbegaun, B.O., Simmons, J.S.G. A BIBLIOGRAPHICAL GUIDE TO THE RUSSIAN LANGUAGE. Oxford, Clarendon Press, 1953.

A practical bibliography for teachers of the Russian language is:

Schaller, H.W. BIBLIOGRAPHIE ZUR RUSSISCHEN SPRACHE. Frankfurt am Main, Lang, 1980 (Symbolae Slavicae, 8).

4.7. Indexes

The bulk of literature in linguistics appears in specialized journals. Subject bibliographies cover it well. Consequently the indexes to journals are less important in linguistics than in other disciplines. The existing indexes usually include both language and literature and therefore Part II.3.5. should be consulted.

4.8. Bibliography of dictionaries

A current bibliography is:

BIBLIOGRAPHIE DER WÖRTERBUCHER ERSCHIENENE IN DER DEUTSCHEN DEMOKRATISCHEN REPUBLIK, RUMÄNISCHEN VOLKSREPUBLIK, TSCHECHOSLOWAKAISCHEN SOZIALISTISCHEN REPUBLIK, UNGARISCHEN VOLKSREPUBLIK, UNION DER SOZIALISTISCHEN SOWJETREPUBLIKEN, VOLKSREPUBLIK BULGARIEN, VOLKSREPUBLIK CHINA. VOLKSREPUBLIK POLEN, 1945-1961 (title also in English, Polish, Russian). Warszawa, Wydawnictwo Naukowo-Techniczne, 1965- The next volume was published in 1968 for 1962-1964, then continued every two years. China ceased to contribute beginning with volume 4.

Retrospective historical value:

Aav, Y. RUSSIAN DICTIONARIES AND GLOSSARIES PRINTED IN RUSSIA, 1627-1917. Zug, Inter Documentation Company, 1977 (Bibliotheca Slavica, 10).

Comprehensive:

Izhevskaia, M.G., et. al. SLOVARI, IZDANNYE V SSSR. BIBLIOGRAFICHESKII UKAZATEL'. 1918-1962 G. Moscow, Nauka, 1966.

Selective:

Lewański, R.C. BIBLIOGRAPHY OF SLAVIC DICTIONARIES. 2nd edition. Bologna, Editrice Compositori, 1973. Volume 3 and a supplementary volume, 4, cover Russian dictionaries.

Zalewski, W. RUSSIAN-ENGLISH DICTIONARIES WITH AIDS FOR TRANSLATORS. A SELECTED BIBLIOGRAPHY. New York, Russica Publishers, 1981 (RUSSICA BIBLIOGRAPHY SERIES, 1) which includes also selected monolingual dictionaries, non-linguistic dictionaries (abbreviations, gazetteers, personal names, pseudonymes, etc. and bibliographies of dictionaries). For an update of this bibliography see RUSSIAN REVIEW, 2, 1983: 215-216.

See also E.V. Gol'tseva, op. cit.

Specialized dictionaries are covered by:

Kaufman, I.M. TERMINOLOGICHESKIE SLOVARI. BIBLIOGRAFIIA. Moscow, Sovetskaia Rossiia, 1961. It covers the period 1704 to 1960.

Bibliography of dictionaries can be found in linguistic bibliographies such as Stankewicz and Unbegaun. The latter is widely annotated and gives excellent information about major monolingual dictionaries of the Russian language. There are also English language bibliographies of dictionaries which include the Russian language. Some of them are annotated. For information about them see Sheehy, op. cit. or Zalewski, op. cit.

5. Social sciences

Most of the fields listed below have their specialized encyclopedias (see Part I. 5.2.2.). Their articles on bibliography will provide good bibliographic guidance.

See also I.K. Kirpicheva, op. cit.;
E.V. Ienish, op. cit.;
INION's bibliographies especially BILIOGRAFICHESKII UKAZATEL'...

5.1. Social sciences in general

BIBLIOGRAFIIA OBSHCHESTVENNO-POLITICHESKOI LITERATURY. UCHEBNIK. L.A. Levin, et. al., eds. Moscow, Kniga, 1968- 1976. 2 vols.

Arkhipova, M.K. TEKUSHCHAIA BIBLIOGRAFIIA OBSHCHESTVENNO-POLITICHESKOI LITERATURY. UCHEBNOE POSOBIE DLIA STUDENTOV BIBLIOTECHNYKH FAKULTETOV. Leningrad, 1974.

UKAZATEL' BIBLIOGRAFICHESKIKH POSOBII PO OBSHCHESTVENNYM NAUKAM. Kiev, AN USSR, 1973-

Oleinik, N.I., et al. RAZVITIE OBSHCHESTVENNYKH NAUK V SSSR. BIBLIOGRAFICHESKII UKAZATEL'. 1967-1979 GG. Kiev, Naukova Dumka, 1983,

See also Part II. 1.1.

5.2. Archeology

Kopylova, V.N. ARKHEOLOGIIA SSSR. ANNOTIROVANNYI UKAZATEL' BIBLIOGRAFII NA RUSSKOM IAZYKE. VYPUSK 1. OBSHCHII OTDEL'. Moscow, 1965.

SOVETSKAIA ARKHEOLOGICHESKAIA LITERATURA. BIBLIOGRAFIIA. Leningrad, AN SSSR (later Nauka), 1959-
1918-1940 in 1965;
1941-1957 in 1959;
1958-1962 in 1969;
1963-1967 in 1975 and the continuation in five-year volumes.

5.3. Ethnography

Titova, Z.D. ETNOGRAFIIA. BIBLIOGRAFIIA RUSSKIKH BIBLIOGRAFII PO ETNOGRAFII NARODOV SSSR, 1851-1969. Moscow, Kniga, 1970.

5.4. Economy

Bibliography of bibliographies:

Sivolgin, V.E. EKONOMIKA SSSR. ANNOTIROVANNYI UKAZATEL' OTECHESTVENNYKH BIBLIOGRAFICHESKIKH POSOBII ZA 1817-1977 GG. 2nd rev. and enlarged ed. Moscow, [MBP], 1979.

Sivolgin, V.E. POLITICHESKAIA EKONOMIA, ISTORIIA EKONOMICHESKOI MYSLI. ANNOTIROVANNYI UKAZATEL' OTECHESTVENNYKH BIBLIOGRAFICHESKIKH POSOBII, IZDANNYKH V 1812-1972 GG. Moscow, [MBP], 1974.

There is a variety of retrospective bibliographies, most of which can be found through Sivolgin, op. cit. We may recall the bibliographies published by INION (see Part II. 1.1. EKONOMICHESKAIA ISTORIIA and NARODNOE KHOZIAISTVO).

The following may also be added as examples:

BIBLIOGRAFIIA PO VOPROSAM POLITICHESKOI EKONOMII, 1917-1975 GG. Moscow, Universitet, 1969-1980. 2 vols.

FINANSY, DEN'GI I KREDIT SSSR, 1946-1966 GG. Moscow, Ministerstvo Finansov, 1967; for 1967-1975 in 1977.

Maliarov, O.I., Shil'dkret, E.A. BIBLIOGRAFICHESKII UKAZATEL' OTECHESTVENNYKH BIBLIOGRAFII PO OKHRANE TRUDA (1890-1971). Leningrad, 1973.

5.5. Education

Bibliography of bibliographies:

Tsybina, O.D., et al. NARODNOE OBRAZOVANIE. PEDAGOGICHESKIE NAUKI. ANNOTIROVANNYI UKAZATEL' OTECHESTVENNYKH BIBLIOGRAFICHESKIKH POSOBII NA RUSSKOM IAZYKE, OPUBLIKOVANNYKH S SEREDINY XIX V. PO 1978 G. Moscow, [MPB], 1981.

Current bibliography:

LITERATURA PO PEDAGOGICHESKIM NAUKAM I NARODNOMU OBRAZOVANIIU. TEKUSHCHII BIBLIOGRAFICHESKII UKAZATEL'. Moscow, 1950- quarterly.

See also Part II.1.1.

Retrospective bibliographies:

Andreeva, E.P., et al. PEDAGOGICHESKAIA BIBLIOGRAFIIA. Moscow, Pedagogika. Published to date: Vol 1: 1924-1930 in 1967.
Vol. 2: 1931-1935 in 1970.
Vol. 3: 1937-1940 in 1937.
Vol. 4: 1941-1949 Vyp. 1.2 in 1983.

Piskunov, A.I. SOVETSKAIA ISTORIKO-PEDAGOGICHESKAIA LITERATURA, 1918-1957. SISTEMATICHESKII UKAZATEL'. Moscow, Akademiia pedagogicheskikh nauk RSFSR, 1960.

Dneprov, E.D. SOVETSKAIA LITERATURA PO ISTORII SHKOLY I PEDAGOGIKI DOREVOLIUTSIONNOI ROSSII, 1918-1977. Moscow, NII obshchei pedagogiki APN SSSR, 1979.

5.6. Law

with Nellie Houke

5.6.1. Bibliography of bibliographies and reference works

Butler, W.E. RUSSIAN AND SOVIET LAW. AN ANNOTATED CATALOG OF REFERENCE WORKS, LEGISLATION, COURT REPORTS, SERIALS AND MONOGRAPHS ON RUSSIAN AND SOVIET LAW (INCLUDING INTERNATIONAL LAW). Zug, Inter Documentation Company, 1976. (BIBLIOTHECA SLAVICA, 8).

Ksenzova, T.E. IURIDICHESKAIA LITERATURA. ANNOTIROVANNYI UKAZATEL' OTECHESTVENNYKH BIBLIOGRAFICHESKIKH POSOBII, IZDANNYKH V 1831-1970 GG. Moscow, Kniga, 1972.

Antonov, V.V. SOVETSKOE ZAKONODATEL'STVO. SPRAVOCHNIK-PUTEVODITEL' PO OSNOVNYM IZDANIIAM. Moscow, Kniga, 1981.

See also Zaionchkovskii, op. cit.

5.6.2. Pre-revolutionary law

Povorinskii, A.F. SISTEMATICHESKII UKAZATEL' RUSSKOI LITERATURY PO GRAZHDANSKOMU PRAVU. 2nd ed. St.Petersburg, Pravitel'stvuiushchii Senat, 1904.

Povorinski, A.F. SISTEMATICHESKII UKAZATEL' RUSSKOI LITERATURY PO SUDOUSTROITEL'STVU I SUDOPROIZVODSTVU GRAZHDANSKOMU I UGOLOVNOMU. St.Petersburg, Pravitel'stvuiushchii Senat, 1896.

Grabar', V.E. MATERIALY K ISTORII LITERATURY MEZHDUNARODNOGO PRAVA V ROSSII. 1647-1917. Moscow, AN SSSR, 1958.

See also Zaionchkovskii, op. cit.

5.6.3. Soviet law

Research and publication in juridical sciences
by Nelli Houke

(Adapted from OCHERKI PO ISTORII IURIDICHESKIKH NAUCHNYKH UCHREZHDENII V SSSR. Moscow, Nauka, 1976: 3-8 and J.-G. Collignon, LES JURISTES EN UNION SOVIETIQUE. Paris, Centre National de la Reserche Scientifique, 1977).

The development of Soviet legal studies, like that of other social sciences, formally began in 1919, when the Central Executive Committee of the RSFSR established the Socialist Academy. They intended it as a center for the construction of a new scholarly establishment based on Marxist principles. Within the Academy (renamed the Communist Academy in 1924) they created the Institute of Soviet Construction and Law in 1929, to concentrate on legal questions. The Russian Association for Scientific Research in Social Sciences (RANION), created in 1920 under the University of Moscow, merged into the Institute in 1930.

By the mid-1930's, when basic Soviet doctrines had been established, the Communist Academy was disbanded. Its Institute for Soviet Construction and Law was absorbed into the Academy of Sciences, and in 1960 became the Institute of State and Law. As of 1975 the Institute employed 250 research personnel in 25 areas of study.

Though the USSR Academy of Sciences is the main research center of the Soviet Union, other institutions carry on active work on legal questions. The juridical research institutes of the republic Academies of Sciences mainly address theoretical issues. The All-Union Research Institute of Soviet Legislation, under the Ministry of Justice, and All-Union Institute for the Study of the Causes and Working Out of Measures for the Prevention of Criminality, under the Procuracy, have existed under various names since the creation of their predecessor, the State Institute for the Study of Criminality and the Criminal, by the NKVD in 1925. These two institutes study more practical problems than do the Academies of Sciences. Similar questions are addressed by the Institute of the

Procuracy -- formed in 1963 to succeed the Procuracy's All-Union Institute of Scientific Study on Criminology -- which now employs 150 research personnel. It publishes the journal VOPROSY BOR'BY S PRETUPNOSTI'IU, 1965-. The Ministry of Public Health has a Central Institute of Forensic Medicine. The Ministry of Internal Affairs administers the Institute of the Police. The Central Research Institute of Judiciary Expertise coordinates the training of experts in criminological techniques. Finally, the Serbskii Research Institute of Legal Psychiatry is known abroad of its involvement in the confinement of political dissidents in psychiatric hospitals.

Judicial publication is coordinated by the publishing house "Iuridicheskaia literatura," created in 1919 and now under the Council of Ministers of the USSR. Other publishers, such as "Nauka" and "Mezhdunarodnye otnosheniia," put out some works on law.

Periodical for specialists is SOVETSKOE GOSUDARSTVO I PRAVO, 1930- organ of the Institut Gosudarstva i Prava of the USSR Academy of Sciences. It supresedes SOVETSKOE PRAVO (1922-1928) and REVOLUTSIIA PRAVA (1927-1929) and appeared under varying title: SOVETSKOE GOSUDARSTVO I REVOLIUTSIIA PRAVA (1930-1932), SOVETSKOE GOSUDARSTVO (1933-1938), SOVETSKOE GOSUDARSTVO I PRAVO (1938-1941). It was suspended in 1941-1945. The more practical journals are SOVETSKAIA ISUTITSIIA, 1922- (title varied), under the Ministry of Justice, SOTSIALISTICHESKAIA ZAKONNOST', 1934- (title varied) edited by IZVESTIIA and administered by the Procuracy and the Supreme Court, and various republican journals. The Supreme Courts and Supreme Soviets of the USSR and the RSFSR, and the Universities of Moscow and Leningrad, put out regular BULLETINS.

The first forty years of Soviet legal scholarship were dominated by the theories of Andrei I. Vyshinskii, who "overemphasized the role of compulsion and underestimated the role of education and prevention..." (GREAT SOVIET ENCYCLOPEDIA. 3rd. ed. New York, Macmillan, 1974, Vol. 4, p. 642). However, since the reform of research institutions in 1963, the field has broadened to include such methods as cybernetics, mathematical models, and comparative legal studies.

Yet, Collignon maintains (op. cit., pp. 131-132) that the research establishment still follows well-worn path, discouraging the exploration of less documented fields such as labor and agricultural law, administrative organization and military law. Nevertheless, the conditions for legal research are improving. Better coordination is limiting duplication of effort, and scholars are increasingly called upon to share their knowledge with legal practitionares.

Bibliographies

Asknazii, F.M., Marshalova, N.V. SOVETSKOE UGOLOVNOE PRAVO. BIBLIOGRAFIIA. 1917-1960. Moscow, Gosiurizdat, 1961, continned by

Gorelik, A.S. SOVETSKOE UGOLOVNOE PRAVO. BIBLIOGRAFICHESKII SPRAVOCHNIK. 1961-1980. Moscow, Iurizdat, 1983.

Dragomiratskaia, K. Ia., et al. SOVETSKOE GRAZHDANSKOE PRAVO. SOVETSKOE SEMEINOE PRAVO. BIBLIOGRAFIIA. 1917-1960 GG. Moscow, Gosiurizdat, 1962.

TRUDOVOE PRAVO. BIBLIOGRAFICHESKII UKAZATEL' OTECHESTVENNOI LITERATURY ZA 1977-1982 GG. Minsk, Pravitel'stvennaia biblioteka, 1981-1983. 3 parts.

Fel'dman, D.I. MEZHDUNARODNOE PRAVO. BIBLIOGRAFIIA. 1917-1972 GG. Moscow, Iurizdat, 1976.

Cameron, G.D. THE SOVIET LAWYER AND HIS SYSTEM. A HISTORICAL AND BIBLIOGRAPHIC STUDY. Ann Arbor, Division of Research, Graduate School of Business Administration, University of Michigan, 1978. (MICHIGAN INTERNATIONAL BUSINESS SERIES, 14).

Academic textbooks

Academic textbooks are published frequently by major academic institutions as well as by Iuridicheskaia literatura. The examples listed below are published by the Iuridicheskaia literatura unless otherwise indicated.

SOVETSKOE ADMINISTRATIVNOE PRAVO. 1981.

SOVETSKOE FINANSOVOE PRAVO. 1982.

SOVETSKOE GOSUDARSTVENNOE PRAVO. 1971. 1974. 1978. 1980. 1983.

SOVETSKOE GRAZHDANSKOE PRAVO. 1965. 1974. 1980. 2 vols.

SOVETSKOE KONSTITUTSIONNOE PRAVO. Leningrad, Universitet, 1975.

SOVETSKOE PENSIONNOE PRAVO. 1974.

SOVETSKOE PRAVO. 1969. 1975. 1980.

SOVETSKOE SEMEINOE PRAVO. 1982.

SOVETSKOE TRUDOVOE PRAVO. 1970. 1976. 1980. 1982.

SOVETSKOE UGOLOVNOE PRAVO. 1973. 1981.

SOVETSKOE ZEMEL'NOE PRAVO. 1965. 1977. 1981.

5.7. Sociology

See Part II.1.1.

6. The Humanities (other than history, literature, language)

6.1. Art

Morozova, L.A. IZOBRAZITEL'NOE ISKUSSTVO. SPRAVOCHNYE I BIBLIOGRAFICHESKIE IZDANIIA. ANNOTIROVANNYI BIBLIOGRAFICHESKII UKAZATEL'. Moscow, Kniga, [MBP], 1982. (A fundamental guide).

Zubov, Iu. S., et, al. BIBLIOGRAFIIA ISKUSSTVA. UCHEBNIK. Moscow, Kniga, 1973.

Krontale, I. PUTEVODITEL' PO BIBLIOGRAFII ISKUSSTVA. Riga, Gos. Biblioteka Latvijskoi SSR, 1975.

Ostroi, O.S. RUSSKIE SPRAVOCHNYE IZDANIIA PO IZOBRAZITEL'NOMU I PRIKLADNOMU ISKUSSTVU. Moscow, Kniga, 1972.

Ostroi, O.S. IZOBRAZITEL'NOE I PRIKLADNOE ISKUSSTVO. BIBLIOGRAFIIA RUSSKOI BIBLIOGRAFII. Moscow, Kniga, 1969.

Important bibliographies are often included in monographs. Such listings can be found in:

Grabar', I., et al., eds. ISTORIIA RUSSKOGO ISKUSSTVA. 2nd ed. Moscow, AN SSSR, 1953-1969. 13 vols. in 15 parts.

Special bibliography is

Senkevitch, A. SOVIET ARCHITECTURE, 1917-1962. A BIBLIOGRAPHICAL GUIDE TO SOURCE MATERIAL. Charlottesville, University Press of Virginia, 1974.

An example of a collection catalog is

Zharkova, I.M., et al. GOSUDARSTVENNAIA TRET'IAKOVSKAIA GALEREIA. KATALOG XVIII-NACHALA XX VEKA (DO 1917 GODA). Moscow, Izobrazitel'noe Iskusstvo, 1984.

6.2. Theater, drama

Drama as a literary genre is best identified through literary bibliographies among which Kandel''s bibliography of bibliographies will be the primary source. The bibliographies listed below focus on the theater as on a cultural and artistic institution.

Histories of theater:

Petrova, V.F. MATERIALY K ISTORII TEATRAL'NOI KUL'-TURY ROSSII XVIII-XX VV. ANNOTIROVANNYI KATALOG. Leningrad, [SS], 1980-

ISTORIIA SOVETSKOGO DRAMATICHESKOGO TEATRA. A. Anastas'ev, et al., eds. Moscow, Nauka, 1966-1971. 6 vols.

Kaneva, E., Strutinskaia, E. GOSUDARSTVENNYI ORDENA LENINA I ORDENA OKTIABR'SKOI REVOLIUTSII AKADE-MICHESKII MALYI TEATR SSSR, 1824-1974. Moscow, Vserossiiskoe teatral'noe obshchestvo, 1978-. (Containisg repertoires, names of administrators and artists, etc.)

Petrovskaia, I.F. MATERIALY K ISTORII RUSSKOGO TEATRA V GOSUDARSTVENNYKH ARKHIVAKH SSSR. OBZOR DOKUMENTOV. XVII V. -1917 G. Moscow, 1966.

Bibliography of bibliographies:

Voksanian, E.A, et al. TEATR. ANNOTIROVANNYI UKAZA-TEL' SPRAVOCHNYKH I BIBLIOGRAFICHESKIKH IZDANII NA RUSSKOM I INNOSTRANNYKH IAZYKAKH (XIX-XX VV). Moscow,[MBP], 1983.

Levina, L.R., et al. RUSSKII SOVETSKII DRAMATICHESKII TEATR. ANNOTIROVANNYI UKAZATEL' BIBLIOGRAFICHESKIKH I SPRAVOCHNYKH MATERIALOV. 1917-1973. Moscow, [Gos. tsentral'naia teatral'-naia biblioteka], 1977-1978. 3 vols.

Berezkin, V.I. SOVETSKAIA LITERATURA PO STSENOGRAFII (1917-1983). SOVIET LITERATURE ON SCENOGRAPHY. KATALOG. Moscow, VIO Gosizopropa-ganda, 1983.

Current bibliography:

EZHEGODNIK P'ES. Moscow, [Gos. tsentral'naia teatral'naia biblioteka], 1975-

See also Part II.1.2.

Others:

Levina, L.R. GOSUDARSTVENNAIA TSENTRAL'NAIA TEATRAL'NAIA BIBLIOTEKA. ANNOTROVANNYI UKAZATEL' RABOT. 1958-1982. Moscow, 1982.

Zernitskaia, E.I., ed. SOVETSKII TEATR DLIA DETEI, 1918-1972. UKAZATEL' LITERATURY. Moscow, [MBP], 1978. 3 vols.

Vishnevskii, V.E. TEATRAL'NAIA PERIODIKA. BIBLIOGRAFICHESKII UKAZATEL':
Chast' 1. 1774-1917;
Chast' 2. 1917-1940. Moscow-Leningrad, Iskusstvo, 1941.

Dana, H.W.L. HANDBOOK ON SOVIET DRAMA: LISTS OF THEATRES, PLAYS, OPERAS, FILMS AND BOOKS AND ARTICLES ABOUT THEM. New York, The American Russian Institute for Cultural Relations with the Soviet Union, Inc. 1938.

6.3. Music

Bibliography of bibliographies:

Koltypina, G.B. BIBLIOGRAFIIA MUZYKAL'NOI BIBLIOGRAFII. ANNOTIROVANNYI PERECHEN' UKAZATELEI LITERATURY, IZDANNOI NA RUSSKOM IAZYKE. Moscow, 1963.

Pavlova, N.G. BIBLIOGRAFIIA MUZYKAL'NOI BIBLIOGRAFII. ANNOTIROVANNYI PERECHEN' UKAZATELEI LITERATURY, IZDANNOI NA RUSSKOM IAZYKE, 1962-1967 GG. Moscow, 1970.

Pavlova, N.G. UKAZATEL' BIBLIOGRAFICHESKIKH POSOBII PO MUZYKE. ANNOTIROVANNYI PERECHEN' UKAZATELEI, IZDANNYKH NA RUSSKOM IAZYKE, 1968-1975 GG. Moscow, 1978.

Stud'ia, E.S. "Iz istorii russkoi muzykal'noi bibliografii", SBORNIK TRUDOV. Moskovskii Institut Kul'tury 22, 1972: 385-411.

Current bibliography:

Startsev, I. SOVETSKAIA LITERATURA O MUZYKE. 1918-1947. BIBLIOGRAFICHESKII UKAZATEL' KNIG. Moscow, Sovetskii Kompozitor, 1963- . (From 1948-1953- title varies, compilers change, coverage expands to include periodical literature).

Koltypina, G.B., Pavlova, N.G. SOVETSKAIA LITERATURA O MUZYKE. BIBLIOGRAFICHESKII UKAZATEL' KNIG, ZHURNAL'NYKH STATEI I RETSENZII ZA 1968-1970 GG. Moscow, Sovetskii kompozitor, 1979-

MUZYKA. BIBLIOGRAFICHESKAIA INFORMATSIIA, op. cit., (see Part II.1.2).

Others:

Batser, D.M., Rabinovich, B.I. RUSSKAIA NARODNAIA MUZYKA. NOTOGRAFICHESKII UKAZATEL' (1776-1973). Moscow, 1981-

Bernandt, G.B. SLOVAR' OPER, VPERVYE POSTAVLENNYKH ILI IZDANNYKH V DOREVOLIUTSIONNOI ROSSII I V SSSR. 1736-1959. Moscow, Sovetskii kompozitor, 1962.

Livanova, T.N. MUZYKAL'NAIA BIBLIOGRAFIIA RUSSKOI PERIODICHESKOI PECHATI XIX V. Moscow, 1960-

Kasatkina, M.Kh. "Ukazateli notnykh izdanii v SSSR," SOVETSKAIA BIBLIOGRAFIIA 2,1977: 27-40.

A series of catalogs:

NOTNYE IZDANIIA V FONDAKH GOSUDARSTVENNOI BIBLIOTEKI SSSR IMENI V.I. LENINA:
For list of catalogs published until 1983 see

NOTNYE IZDANIIA V FONDAKH GOSUDARSTVENNOI BIBLIOTEKI SSSR IMENI LENINA. KATALOG.FORTEPIANO. UCHEBNO-PEDAGOGICHESKII REPERTUAR. SOVETSKIE NOTNYE IZDANIIA, 1970-1980 GG. Moscow, MBP, 1983.

Non-bibliographic references:

Koltypina, G.B. SPRAVOCHNAIA LITERATURA PO MUZYKE: SLOVARI, SBORNIKI, BIOGRAFII, KALENDARI, KHRONIKI, PAMIATNYE KNIZHKI, PUTEVODITELI, SBORNIKI LIBRETTO, SBORNIKI TSITAT. UKAZATEL' IZDANII NA RUSSKOM IAZYKE, 1773-1962 GG. Moscow, Kniga, 1964.
continued for 1963-1970 in 1972;
1971-1978 in 1980.

6.4. Film

Current bibliography:

EZHEGODNIK KINO for years 1955-1961 had: "Daty i fakty; Fil'mografiia; Bibliografiia." Its continuation: EKRAN has only "Fil'mografiia."

Retrospective:

SOVETSKIE KHUDOZHESTVENNYE FIL'MY. ANNOTIROVANNYI KATALOG. 1918-1957. Moscow, Iskusstvo, 1961. 3 vols. and continuation. Latest volume published for 1964-1975 in 1975.

KNIGI O KINO, 1917-1960 GG. ANNOTIROVANNAIA BIBLIOGRAFIIA. Moscow, Institut istorii iskusstv, 1962.

Cohen, L.H. THE SOVIET CINEMA, FILM AND PHOTOGRAPHY. A SELECTED ANNOTATED BIBLIOGRAPHY. Revised ed. Edwards Air Force Base, CA., 1976.

Leyda J. "Seventy five years of Russian and Soviet films, 1907-1982. A Select list," KINO. A HISTORY OF THE RUSSIAN AND SOVIET FILM. 3rd ed. Princeton, N.J., Princeton University Press, 1983.

Bibliographic information can be found in:

ISTORIIA SOVETSKOGO KINO, 1917-1967. Kh. Abul-Kasymov, et al., eds. Moscow, Iskusstvo, 1969-1978. 4 vols.

See also Part I. 5.3.7.

6.5. Philosophy

Isachenkova, A.I. RETROSPEKTIVNAIA BIBLIOGRAFIIA PO FILOSOFII I NAUCHNOMU KOMMUNIZMU. UCHEBNOE POSOBIE. Leningrad, 1973.

See also Part II. 1.1., and

J.S.G. Simmons, op. cit., pp. 51-52.

6.6 Religion

Donzhina, T.I. BIBLIOGRAFICHESKIE UKAZATELI I SPRAVOCHNIKI PO VOPROSAM ATEIZMA, ISTORII I KRITIKI RELIGII. L'vov, Universitet, 1964.

Grekulov, E.F. BIBLIOGRAFICHESKII UKAZATEL' LITERATURY PO ISSLEDOVANIIU PRAVOSLAVIIA, STAROOBRIADCHESTVA I SEKTANTSTVA V SOVETSKOI ISTORICHESKOI NAUKE, 1922-1972 GG. Moscow, 1974-
1973-1975 in 1976-1977;
1976 in 1977;
1977 in 1979.

See also J.S.G. Simmons, op. cit., pp. 52-55.

NAME INDEX

Aav, Y., 141
Abramov, K.I., 26
Abramovich, D.N., 123
Abul-Kasymov, Kh., 154
Adariukov, V.Ia., 5
Adams, A.E., 111
Ado, A.V., 104
Alatortseva, A.I., 104, 111
Al'bitskii, A.P., 123
Alekseeva, G.D., 111
Alferova, L.N., 11
Amburger, E., 111
Amirova, T.A., 136
Anastas'ev, A., 151
Anastasevich, V.G., 13, 15, 54
Andreeva, E.P., 47,144
Andreeva, N.F., 59
Andreevskii, I.E., 69
Antonov, V.V., 145
Ariskevich, N.P., 83
Arkhipova, M.K., 43, 142
Arsen'ev, K.K., 69
Ashnin, F.D., 137
Asknazii, F.M., 148
Astrakhantseva, I.F.,107
Auty, A., 7
Avilova, N.S., 140

Bakhtin, V.S., 76
Bakst, E.I., 98
Bakunina, I.A., 34
Balashova, L.P., 39
Bamborschke, K., 130,131
Bannikova, N.P., 94, 133
Barenbaum, I.E., 7,9, 43
Barsuk, A.J., 11, 23
Barykina, O.A., 88
Baskakov, V.N., 117
Batser, D.M., 153
Bazunov, A.F.,14, 55, 101
Bel'chikov, N.F., 31
Belinskii, V.G., 15, 116
Belov, G.A., 22, 36, 37
Belov, S.V., 8, 123
Berezin, F.M., 136
Berezkin, V.I., 151
Berkov, P.N., 120
Bernandt, G.B., 78, 153
Besterman, T.A., 47
Birkos, A.S., 60, 77
Bodnarskii, B.S., 12, 18, 20, 21, 47
Boer, S.P. (de), 74
Boldov, V.B., 82
Bonnières, F. (de), 45, 65
Brainina, B. Ia., 76
Brang, P., 139
Briskman, M.A., 12, 21, 43, 52
Brown, A., 70
Brown, J.H., 39
Bukhstab, B. Ia., 21, 120, 123, B.Ia., 32,
Bulich, S.K., 136
Butler, W.E., 145
Butrin, M., 76
Bykova, N.M., 88
Bykova, T.A., 32

Cameron, G.D., 148
Catherine II, 114
Chekhov, A.P., 116
Cherepakov, M.S., 59
Chernenko, R.D., 77
Chernevskii, P.O.,78

Chernomorskii, M.N., 107
Chernyshevskii, N.G., 15, 116
Chew, A.F., 111
Clarke, R.A., 81
Cohen, L.H., 154
Collignon, J.-G., 146,148
Crowther, P.A., 109

Dana, H.W.L., 152
Davydova, T.E., 7
Debets, N.P., 137,138
Dement'ev, A.B., 59
Demidov, P., 13
Diomidova, G.N., 11, 43
Djaparidze, D., 31
Dmitreva, R.P., 22, 108, 122
Dneprov, E.D., 144
Dobroliubov, N.A., 15, 116
Dolmatovskaia, G.E., 77
Dolzhanskii, A., 78
Donzhina, T.I., 155
Doronin, I.P., 103
Dossick, J.J., 61
Dostoevskii, F., 116
Dragomiratskaia, K.Ia.,148
Dremina, G.A., 38
Drobizhev, V.Z., 108, 111
Droblenkova, N.F., 22, 122, 129

Ebin, P.E., 121
Eikhengol'ts, A.D., 11, 18, 21, 43
Efremov, P.A., 14, 54
Egorova, L.E., 8
Eitmontova, R.G., 106
Eroshkin, N.P., 112
Erzin, S.A., 121
Esin, B.I., 58
Ettinger, A., 130

Fedosova, I.A., 107
Fel'dman, D.I., 148
Fomin, A.G., 20, 121
Foster, L., 132
Fradkina, Z.L., 99, 100
Friedland, A.P., 84
Franz, E., 126
Fursenko, L.I., 29

Galin, G.A., 40
Garnier, E.A., 109
Garshina, N.A., 35
Gel'fand, N., 120, 123
Gertsen, A.I., 116
Ghabat, M.Ts., 138
Gibian, G., 130
Gilbert, M., 111
Gillula, J.W., 81
Girke, W., 139
Gladstone, J.M., 130
Glavatskikh, G.A., 97, 98, 102, 104, 106
Glazunov, I.I., 14, 55, 101
Gogol', N., 116
Goldberg, A.L., 64, 98
Goldberg, V.V., 118
Golovkin, A., 13
Gol'tseva, E.V., 13, 68, 141
Golubeva, O.D., 126
Gorelik, A.S., 148
Gorfein, G.M., 38
Gor'kii, M., 116
Gorokhoff, B.I., 7
Goslett, P.C., 130
Govorov, A.A., 7
Gozulov, A.I., 81
Grabar', I., 150
Grabar', V.I., 145
Gracheva, I.B., 49, 51
Grant, S.A., 39
Grebenshchikov, I.P.,20
Grech', N.I., 15

Grechushnikova, D.B., 29
Grekulov, E.F., 155
Grierson, P., 64
Grigor'ev, V.N., 79
Grimsted, P.K., 31, 33, 38
Grossman, Iu.M., 37

Hansack, E., 131
Heiliger, W., 73
Hellmann, M., 109
Hodnett, G., 75
Horak, S.M., 44
Horecky, P.L., 44
Hoskins, J.W., 34, 65
Howell, D.L.L., 45

Iakovlev, M., 77
Iakovleva, I.G., 64, 98
Ianitskii, N.F., 18
Ianovskii, A.E., 12,
Ienish, E.V., 43, 44, 192
Ikonnikov, V.S., 36, 106
In'kova, L.M., 27
Isachenkova, A.I., 155
Isakov, Ia.A., 14, 55, 101
Iskol'dskaia, K.K., 103
Iuzhakov, S.N., 69
Izhevskaia, M.G., 141

Jagić, I.V., 136
Jones, D.L., 65, 73

Kaiser, E., 131
Kalent'eva, A.G., 119
Kamentseva, E.I., 111
Kandel', B.L., 1, 12, 23, 44, 46, 53, 120, 121, 124, 132, 151
Kaneva, E., 151
Karataev, S.I., 79
Karavaev, V.F., 79
Karskii, E.F., 6
Kartashov, N.S., 23
Kasabova, B.N., 11
Kasack, W., 75
Kasatkina, M.Kh., 153
Kaufman, I.M., 21, 68, 70, 73, 82, 141
Kerner, R.J., 64, 65
Khar'kova, A.M., 27
Khaskelis, M.L., 103
Khotin, L., 67
Kim, M.P., 7
Kiprianov, V., 13
Kirpicheva, I.K., 42, 43, 142
Kleimenova, R.W., 126
Kochetkova, N., 33
Kochetov, F., 13
Kolchynina, Z.I., 29
Kolesnikova, M.I., 133
Kolosova, E.V., 38
Koltypina, G.B., 152, 154
Kopylova, V.N., 142
Korneev, S.G., 76
Korotkina, B.M., 139
Korshunov, O.P., 11, 12, 19, 23, 43
Koschmieder, E., 139
Kotkov, S.I., 135
Koval'chenko, I.D., 107
Kovalevskii, M.M., 69
Kraevskii, A.A., 15
Kraineva, N.Ia., 97
Krasheninnikov,P.I.,14
Krassovsky, D., 74
Krause, F., 29
Krendel', R.N., 120, 123
Krontale, I., 150
Krupskaia, N., 20
Krylov, I., 114
Ksenzova, I.E., 145
Kufaev, M.N., 20

Kukushkina, E.S., 136
Kutik, V.N., 37
Kuznetsev, I.V., 58

Lambin, B.P. and
Lambin, P.P., 14,
101
Laskeev, N.A., 35
Laufer, Iu. M., 23, 119
Law, A.H., 130
Lebed, A.I., 77
Lebedeva, E.D.,
133
Lenin, 18
Lermontov, M., 116
Lesiuk, E.T., 97
Lesokhina, E.I., 27
Levin, L.A., 142
Levina, L.R., 151, 152
Levshin, B.V., 37
Lewański, R.C., 40,
130, 141
Lewytzkyi, B., 74, 81
Leyda, J., 154
Libman, V.A., 94, 120,
131, 133
Line, M.B., 130
Lisovskii, N.M., 18,
58, 100
Livanova, T.N., 153
Livshits, F.D., 81
Lomonosov, M., 116
Lorkovic, T., 49
Lukianov, A.I., 85
Luppov, S.P., 5, 6, 8, 26
Lur'e, A.N., 76

Maiakovskii, I.L., 36
Maichel, K., 1, 17, 44,
82, 99, 108
Maikov, L., 60
Maksakov, V.V., 36
Maliarov, O.I., 143
Malinskaia, B.A., 137
Malykhin, N.G., 7
Mamontov, A.V., 52, 53
Markus, V.A., 9
Marshalova, N.V., 148
Martynov, I.F., 123
Masanov, Iu. I., 11, 12,
23, 57, 59, 78, 105,
107, 125
Mashikhin, E.A., 79
Mashkova, M.V., 12, 21
Matko, D.J.I., 81
Matsuev, N.I., 20, 75,
123, 126, 127, 129, 139
Maxwell, R., 70
Meier, M.S., 104
Melinskaya, S.I., 77
Mel'ts, M.Ia., 133
Meyer, K., 110
Mez'er, A.V., 5,8,14,18,20,
27,43,47,57,59,87,119,122,
123,129
Mezhov, V.I., 14,64,79,87,
100,101,102,122
Mikhailova, A.K., 117
Mil'chin, A.E., 9
Miliukov, P.N., 69
Miller, T.N., 126
Morely, Ch., 39
Morozova, I.V., 55
Morozova, L.A., 150
Muratova, K.D., 22, 123,
129
Muromtsev, S.A., 69

Naidich, E.E., 133
Nazarov, A.I., 7
Nazarevskii, A.A., 122
Nekrasov, N.A., 15, 116
Nemirovskii, E.L., 6, 8
Nerhood, H.W., 108
Neustroev, A.N., 14, 60
Nevskii, V.I., 20
Nikitin, S.A., 107
Nikitina, E.F., 76
Nizheva, O.N., 34
Nor-Mesek, N., 75
Novikov, N.I., 13, 106,
113, 114

Novikova, N.G., 41

Obolensky, D., 7
Oleinik, N.I., 142
Oogareff, V., 75
Osipov, V.O., 55
Osipova, I.P., 27
Ostroi, O.S., 150
Ozerova, G.A., 53
Oznobishin, D.V., 117

Pachmuss, T., 132
Pavlova, N.G., 152,153
Paxton, J., 111
Penchko, N.A., 27
Peretts, V.P., 122
Petrova, V.F., 151
Petrovskaia, I.F., 151
Piotrovskii, B.B., 5, 8
Piskunov, A.I., 144
Plavil'shchnikov, V.A., 13
Podomazova, T.A., 8, 9
Pohrt, H., 64
Polansky, P., 28
Polevoi, N.A., 15
Polonskaia, M., 33
Popov, V.A., 14, 60
Postnikov, S.P., 65
Povorinskii, A.F., 145
Pozdeeva, V.I., 32
Prokhorov, A.M., 69, 70
Pronina, P.V., 97
Pushkarev, S.G., 111
Pushkin, A.S., 15, 114, 116, 117

Rabinovich, B.F., 153
Radishchev, A., 116
Ravikovich, D., 40
Razumovskii, A., 13
Reshetinskii, I.I., 47
Rieper, W., 75
Rogov, A.I., 31
Rogozhin, N.P., 54
Rozanov, I.N., 20
Rozov, N.N., 5, 6
Rubakin, N.A., 55, 58, 102, 124
Rubinstein, N.L., 106
Rumiantsev, N.P., 107
Ryskin, E.I., 21, 120, 121, 124, 128, 129

Santalov, A.A., 84
Sapunov, B.V., 5
Schaller, H.W., 136, 139, 140
Schatoff, M.V., 66
Schmidt, Ch.D., 110
Schmiegelow-Powell, A., 104, 105
Schultheiss, Th., 65
Seemann,. K.D., 131
Segal, L., 84
Seleznev, M.S., 108
Semenov (Tian-Shanskii), P.P. 83
Sendich, M., 84
Senkevitch, A., 150
Senkovskii, O.I., 14,114
Sergienko, G.V., 28
Seydoux, M., 68
Shamurin, E.I., 20
Shapiro, A.L., 22, 60, 63, 82, 99, 102, 110
Shapiro, D.M., 109
Shcherba, N.M., 52
Sheehy, P., 44, 61, 129, 131, 141
Shepelev, L.E., 38
Shibanov, F.A., 22, 82
Shil'dkret, E.A., 143
Shilova, I., 77
Shilstone, M., 46
Shiperovich, B., 116
Shmidt, O.Iu., 69

Shmushkis, I.E., 68,
Shoup, P.S., 81
Shtein, E., 132
Shvedova, O.I., 106
Sibiriakov, I.M., 101
Sidorov, A.A., 5, 8
Simanovskii, I.B., 20
Simchera, V.M., 79
Simmons, G., 74
Simmons, J.S.G., 1, 7, 17, 31, 39, 45, 61, 133, 140, 155
Sivolgin, V.E., 143
Slukhovskii, M.I., 26
Smirdin, A.F., 14, 54, 114
Smirnov-Sokol'skii, N.P., 33, 118, 126
Sokolovskaia, Z.K., 77
Sokurova, M.V., 21,47,49
Sopikov, V.S., 14, 54
Sorokin, V.V., 27
Späth, M., 110
Sreznevskii, V., 58
Staar, R., 85
Stankiewicz, E., 85, 141
Stan'ko, A.I., 58
Starokadomskaia, M.K.,98
Startsev, I., 153
Stennik, Iu.V., 22, 123
Stepanov, V.P., 22, 33, 79, 123, 126, 129
Stepanova, A.G., 136
Stevens, M., 65
Stroynowski, J., 74
Strutnitskaia, E., 151
Stud'ia, E.S., 153
Sumkina, A.I., 135
Suvorova, A.V., 59
Sworakowski, W., 85
Syrchenko, L.G., 38

Tambs, L.A., 60
Tarasenkov, A., 124
Tatishchev, V.N., 106
Tian-Shanskii, see: Semenov, P.P.
Terry, G.M., 62, 130
Tikhomirov, M.N., 106, 107
Timiriazev, K.A., 69
Titov, A., 53
Titova, Z.D., 53, 1143
Tolstoi, L., 116, 117
Toropov, A.D., 16, 18
Trishkina, N.S., 28
Tropovskii, L.N. 18, 19, 20
Tsybina, O.D., 144
Turgenev, I., 116, 117

Ul'ianinskii, D.V., 33
Ul'ianov, N.A., 60
Unbegaun, B.O., 140, 141
Urban, P.K., 77
Uspenskii, G., 113

Vaisbord, E.A., 106
Valk, S.N., 108
Vaneev, A.N., 27
Vasil'chenko, V.I., 25, 26
Vasmer, M., 83
Vavilov, S.I., 69
Vengerov, S.A., 14, 18, 87, 119, 122, 124
Vezirova, L.A., 119
Vialikov, V.I., 36
Vinogradov, V.A., 88
Vinogradova, L.B., 103
Vishnevskii, V.E., 152

Vitman, A.M., 125
Vladislavlev, I.V., 18, 119, 125
Voksanian, E.A., 151
Volkoff, A.M., 34
Vvedenskii, B.A., 69
Vyshinskii, A.I., 141

Walker, G.P.M., 7, 9, 40, 45, 81, 83
Weber, H.B., 73
Werner, W. 130
Whitby, T.J., 49, 51
Wieczynski, J.L., 73
Winchell, C.W., 44
Woll, J., 66, 132
Worth, D.S., 139
Wynar, L.R., 40
Wytrzens, G., 124, 125, 129, 132

Zaborova, R.B., 38
Zaionchkovskii, P.A., 68, 78, 82, 83, 97, 108, 110, 114, 145
Zakharova, A.S., 82
Zalewski, W., 45, 46, 80, 99, 141
Zapadov, V.A., 33, 57
Zdobnov, N.V.,12, 20, 21, 48, 58
Zernitskaia, E.I., 152
Zernova, A.S., 32
Zharkova, I.M., 150
Zheltova, N.I., 133
Zinin, S.I., 137
Zubov, Iu.S., 150
Züllig, M., 139

APPENDIX

Alla Avisov

SERIALS: TERMINOLOGY AND CURRENT MONOGRAPHIC NUMBERED SERIES PUBLISHED IN THE WEST

TERMINOLOGY

almanakh	miscellanea
biulleten'	bulletin (includes continuing bibliographies)
doklady	reports, addresses, papers, lectures
gazeta	newspaper
izvestiia	news, transactions
otchety	reports
sbornik	collection, symposium, volume of articles
soobshcheniia	reports, information, communication
trudy	works (usually monographs)
uchenye zapiski	notes, transactions, collection of papers and/or monographs.
vedomosti	lists, registers, records, gazette
vestnik	bulletin, messanger [herald]
voprosy	same as sbornik
zapiski	same as uchenye zapiski
zhurnal	journal

CURRENT MONOGRAPHIC NUMBERED SERIES PUBLISHED IN THE WEST

AMERICAN UNIVERSITY STUDIES. SERIES 12. SLAVIC LANGUAGES AND LITERATURE. New York, P. Lang.
ANNALES INSTITUTI SLAVICI. Köln, Böhlau Verlag.
ANNUAIRE RUSSE, UKRAINIEN, BIELORUSSE DE FRANCE. Neudon, France : Foyer St. Georges, Centre d'Etudes Russes.
ARBEITEN UND TEXTE ZUR SLAVISTIK. München, Sagner.
ASTRA; SOVIET AND EAST EUROPEAN BIBLIOGRAPHIES. Nottingham.
BAUSTEINE ZUR GESCHICHTE DER LITERATUR BEI DEN SLAWEN. Bad Homburg, Verlag Gahlen.
BEITRÄGE ZUR GESCHICHTE OSTEUROPAS. Köln, Böhlau.
BEITRÄGE ZUR SLAVISTIK. Frankfurt/Main, P. Lang
BERICHTE DES OSTEUROPA INSTITUTS DER FREIEN UNIVERSITAT. Berlin, Freie Universität, Osteuropa Institut.
BIBLIOGRAPHIC GUIDES OF THE LIBRARY SCHOOL OF SLAVONIC AND EAST EUROPEAN STUDIES. London, University of London.
BIBLIOGRAPHIC SERIES OF THE LIBRARY OF SCHOOL OF SLAVONIC AND EAST EUROPEAN STUDIES. London, University of London.
BIBLIOGRAPHISCHE MITTEILUNGEN DES OSTEUROPA INSTITUTS DER FREIEN UNIVERSITÄT. Berlin, Freie Universität, Osteuropa Institut.
BIBLIOTHECA SLAVICA. Zug, Switzerland, Inter-Documentation Company.
BIBLIOTHECA SLAVONICA. Amsterdam, Hekkert.
BIBLIOTHECA SLAVONICA JUNIORA. Amsterdam, Hekkert.
BIBLIOTHEQUE RUSSE DE L'INSTITUTE D'ÉTUDES SLAVES. Paris, Institute d'études slaves.
BIRMINGHAM SLAVONIC MONOGRAPHS. Birmingham, English Dept. of Russian language and literature. University of Birmingham.
CANTENBURY READERS IN RUSSIAN POETRY. Christchurch, Univ. of Cantenbury, Dept. of Modern languages.
COMPANION TO RUSSIAN STUDIES. Cambridge, University Press.
DESCRIPTION AND ANALYSIS OF CONTEMPORARY STANDARD RUSSIAN. Gravenhagen, Mouton.

DUTCH STUDIES IN RUSSIAN LITERATURE. The Hague, Mouton.
EAST EUROPEAN AREA STUDIES SERIES. Rochester, N. Y., Libraries unlimited.
EAST EUROPEAN BIBLIOGRAPHY SERIES. Newtonville, Mass., Oriental Research Partners.
EAST EUROPEAN BIOGRAPHY SERIES. Newtonville, Mass., Oriental Research Partners
EAST EUROPEAN IN BIBLIOGRAPHIES AND STUDIES SERIES. Mt. Vernon, N. Y., Alfi Publication.
EAST EUROPEAN MONOGRAPHS. Boulder, Colorado.
EAST EUROPEAN SERIES. Ann Arbor, Univ. of Michigan, Dept. of Slavic languages and literatures.
EAST EUROPEAN SERIES: LANGUAGE AND LITERATURE. GROUP 1. DESCRIPTIVE GRAMMARS. London, London Univ. School of Slavonic and East European Studies.
EAST EUROPEAN SERIES: LANGUAGE AND LITERATURE. GROUP 2. HISTORICAL GRAMMARS. London, London University, School of Slavonic and East European Studies.
EAST EUROPEAN SERIES: LANGUAGE AND LITERATURE. GROUP 3. READINGS IN LITERATURE. London, London University, School of Slavonic and East European Studies.
EDITION SLAVICA. Wien, G. Leber Verlag.
ERZIEHUNGSWISSENSCHAFTLICHE VERÖFFENTLICHUNGEN DES OSTEUROPA INSTITUTS DER FREIEN UNIVERSITÄT. Berlin, Freie Universität, Osteuropa Institut.
EUROPA ORIENTALIS. Roma, Italy. Instituto per l'Europa orientalis.
EUROPÄISCHE HOCHSCHULSCHRIFTEN. REIHE 16. SLAVISCHE SPRACHEN UND LITERATUREN. Frankfurt, P. Lang.
FORSCHUNGEN ZUR OSTEUROPÄISCHEN GESCHICHTE DES OSTEUROPA INSTITUTS DER FREIEN UNIVERSITÄT. Berlin, Freie Universität, Osteuropa Institut.
FORUM SLAVICUM. München, W. Fink.
HAMBURGER BEITRÄGE FUR RUSSISCH-LEHRER. Hamburg, Buske.
HARVARD SLAVIC STUDIES. Cambridge, Mass., Harvard University Press.
INDIANA SLAVIC STUDIES. Bloomington, Indiana University.
INNSBRUCKER BEITRÄGE ZUR KULTURWISSENSCHAFT. SLAVICA AENIPONTANA. Innsbruck, AMOE.
KIRCHE IM OSTEN: MONOGRAPHIENREIHE. Göttingen, Vandenhoeck v. Ruprecht.

KLAGENFURTER BEITRÄGE ZUR SPRACHWISSENSCHAFT: SLAWISTISCHE REIHE. Klagenfurt, Klagenfurter Sprachwissenschaftliche Gesellschaft.
LINGUISTIC AND LITERARY STUDIES IN EASTERN EUROPE. Amsterdam, Benjamins.
LUND SLAVONIC MONOGRAPHS. Lund.
MAINZER SLAVISTISCHE VERÖFFENTLICHUNGEN. SLAVICA MOGUNTIACA. Mainz, Lieber Verlag.
MARBURGER OSTFORSCHUNGEN. Marburg, Verlag Holzner.
MARQUETTE SLAVIC STUDIES. Milwaukee, Marquette University.
MICHIGAN SLAVIC CONTRIBUTIONS. Ann Arbor, Univ. of Michigan, Dept. of Slavic Languages and Literatures.
MICHIGAN SLAVIC MATERIALS. Ann Arbor, Univ. of Michigan, Dept. of Slavic Languages and Literatures.
MICHIGAN SLAVIC PUBLICATIONS. BIBLIOGRAPHIC SERIES. Ann Arbor, Univ. of Michigan, Dept. of Slavic Languages and Literatures.
MICHIGAN SLAVIC TRANSLATIONS. Ann Arbor, Univ. of Michigan Dept. of Slavic Languages and Literatures.
MICHIGAN STUDIES IN THE HUMANITIES. Ann Arbor, University of Michigan.
MODERN RUSSIAN LITERATURE AND CULTURE: STUDIES AND TEXTS. Berkeley, Berkeley Slavic Specialists.
MONUMENTA LINGUAE SLAVICAE DIALECTI VETERIS. FONTES ET DISSERTATIONES. Wiesbaden, Harrassowitz.
NEW YORK UNIVERSITY SLAVIC PAPERS. Columbus, Ohio. Slavica Publishers.
O.S.U. SLAVIC PAPERS. Ohio State University. Columbus, Ohio. Slavica Publishers.
OCCASIONAL PAPERS IN SLAVIC LANGUAGES AND LITERATURES. Seattle, Washington, Univ. of Wash.
OPERA SLAVICA. N. F. Wiesbaden, Harrassowitz.
OSTEUROPA UND DER INTERNATIONALE KOMMUNISMUS. Baden-Baden, Nomos Verlag.
OSTEUROPAFORSCHUNG. Berlin, Berlin-Verlag.
OSTEUROPASTUDIEN DER HOCHSCHULEN DES LANDES HESSEN. REIHE 1. GIESSENER ABHANDLUNGEN ZUR AGRAR- UND WISSENSCHAFTSFORSCHUNG DES EUROPÄISCHEN OSTENS. Berlin, In Komm. bei Duncker und Humblot.
OSTEUROPASTUDIEN DER HOCHSCHULEN DES LANDES HESSEN. REIHE 2. MARBURGER ABHANDLUNDEN ZUR GESCHICHTE UND KULTUR OSTEUROPAS. Wiesbaden, Harrassowitz.

OSTEUROPASTUDIEN DER HOCHSCHULEN DES LANDES HESSEN. REIHE 3. FRANKFURTER ABHANDLUNDEN ZUR SLAVISTIK. Wiesbaden, Harrassowitz.
OSTMITTELEUROPA IN VERGANGENHEIT UND GEGENWART. Koln, Bohlau Verlag.
OXFORD SLAVONIC PAPERS. Oxford, Clarendon Press.
OXFORD SLAVONIC PAPERS. NEW SERIES. Oxford, Clarendon Press.
OXFORD RUSSIAN READERS. Oxford, Clarendon Press.
PAPERS OF THE SLAVIC INSTITUTE. Marquette University. Milwaukee, Wisconsin.
PERGAMON OXFORD RUSSIAN SERIES. Oxford, Pergamon Press.
PHILOSOPHISCHE UND SOZIOLOGISCHE VERÖFFENTLICHUNGEN DES OSTEUROPA INSTITUTS DER FREIEN UNIVERSITÄT. Berlin, Freie Universität, Osteuropa Institut.
PUBLICATIONS OF EIGHTEENTH-CENTURY RUSSIAN LITERATURE. Evanstone, Northwestern Univ. Press.
PUBLICATIONS ON RUSSIA AND EASTERN EUROPE OF THE SCHOOL OF INTERNATIONAL STUDIES, UNIV. OF WASHINGTON. Seattle, Univ. of Washington Press.
QUEENS SLAVIC PAPERS. Flashing, N. Y. Queen's College Press.
QUELLEN UND STUDIEN ZUR GESCHICHTE OSTEUROPAS. Berlin, Akademie der Wissenschaften.
QUELLENHEFTE ZUR OSTDEUTSCHEN UND OSTEUROPÄISCHEN KIRCHENGESCHICHTE. Ulm, Donau.
RECHTSWISSENSCHAFTLICHE FOLGE DES OSTEUROPA INSTITUTS DER FREIEN UNIVERSITÄT. Belin, Freie Universität, Osteuropa Institut.
RECHTSWISSENSCHAFTLICHE VERÖFFENTLICHUNGEN DES OSTEUROPA INSTITUTS DER FREIEN UNIVERSITÄT. Berlin, Freie Universität, Osteuropa Institut.
RUSSIA OBSERVED. New York, Arno Press.
RUSSIAN AND EAST EUROPEAN STUDIES. Pittsburgh, Univ. of Pittsburgh Press.
RUSSIAN AND EAST EUROPEAN STUDIES CENTER SERIES. Los Angeles, Russian and East European Studies Center. University of Calif. at Los Angeles.
RUSSIAN AND EAST EUROPEAN SERIES. Bloomington, Indiana University.
RUSSIAN ARCHIVAL SERIES. Russian Institute, Columbia Univ. Newtonville, Ma. Oriental Res. Partners.
RUSSIAN BIOGRAPHY SERIES. Newtonville, Ma. Oriental Research Partners.
RUSSIAN LITERATURE IN TRANSLATION. Albany, State Univ. of New York.

RUSSIAN MEMOIR SERIES. Newtonville, Mass. Oriental Research Partners.
RUSSIAN MEMOIRS. Kingston, Ont., Limestone Press.
RUSSIAN OLD AND NEW SERIES. New York, McMillan.
RUSSIAN POETICS IN TRANSLATION. Oxford, Holden Press.
RUSSIAN REPRINT SERIES. The Hague, Europe Printing.
RUSSIAN RESEARCH CENTER STUDIES. Harvard Univ., Russian Research Center.
RUSSIAN SERIES. Gulf Breeze, Academic International Press.
THE RUSSIAN SERIES. Hattiesburg, Miss., Academic International Press.
RUSSIAN SERIES OF THE INTERNATIONAL INSTITUTE FOR SOCIAL HISTORY. The Hague, Mouton.
RUSSIAN SERIES OF THE CARNEGIE ENDOWMENT FOR INTERNATIONAL PEACE CLASSICS IN RUSSIAN STUDIES SERIES. N.Y.Carnegie endowment for intern. peace.
RUSSIAN STUDY SERIES OF THE RUSSIAN INSTITUTE. Chicago, Russian language specialties.
RUSSIAN TROUGH EUROPEAN EYES. London, Cass.
RUSSIAN TITLE FOR THE SPECIALIST. Letchworth, Herts. Pridraux Press.
RUSSICA BIBLIOGRAPHY SERIES. N. Y., Russica Publ.
SCHRIFTEN DES KOMITETS DER BUNDESREPUBLIK DEUTSCHLAND ZUR FÖRDERUNG DER SLAWISCHEN STUDIEN. Giessen, W. Schmitz Verlag.
SCHRIFTEN ZUR GEISTESGESCHICHTE DES ÖSTLICHEN EUROPA. Wiesbaden, Harrassowitz.
SCHRIFTENREIHE DES REGENSBURGER OSTEUROPA INSTITUTS. Regensburg, Lassleben.
SELECTA SLAVICA. Neuried, Hieronymus.
SLAVIC LITERATURES IN CANADA. Winnipeg, UVAN.
SLAVICA. Venezia, Marsilio.
SLAVICA GANDENSIA. ANALECTA. Ghent, State Univ., Dept. of Slavic philology.
SLAVICA GOTHOBURGENSIA. Stockholm, Almquist and Wiskell.
SLAVICA HELVETICA. Bern, P. Lang.
SLAVICA LUNDENSIA. Lund, Slaviska Institutionen vid Lunds universitet.
SLAVICA OTHINIENSIA. Odense University.
SLAVICA REPRINT. Dusseldorf, Brucken Verlag.
SLAVISCHE BIOGRAPHIEN. München, Trofenik.
SLAVISCHE GESCHICHTSBESCHREIBER. Graz, Styria.
SLAVISCHE PROPYLÄEN; TEXTE IN NEU- UND NACHDRUCKEN. München, Erdos.

SLAVISCHE SPRACHEN UND LITERATUREN. München, Hieronymus Verlag.
SLAVISKA OCH BALTISKA STUDIER. Lund, H. Ohlsson.
SLAVISKE STUDIER. Aarhus, Arkona.
SLAVISTIC PRINTINGS AND REPRINTINGS. The Hague, Mouton.
SLAVISTICA. Winnipeg, Canadian Association of Slavists.
SLAVISTICA. Winnipeg, Ukrains'ka vil'na akademiia nauk.
SLAVISTISCHE ARBEITEN. München, Trofenik.
SLAVISTISCHE BEITRAGE. München, Sagner.
SLAVISTISCHE FORSCHUNGEN. Köln, Böhlau.
SLAVISTISCHE LINGUISTIK. Frankfurt/Main, P. Lang.
SLAVISTISCHE SCHRIFTENBÜCHER. NEUE FOLGE. Wiesbaden, Harrassowitz.
SLAVISTISCHE STUDIENBÜCHER. Wiesbaden, Harrassowitz.
SLAVISTISCHE TEXTE UND STUDIEN. Hildesheim, Olms Verlag.
DIE SLAWISCHEN SPRACHEN. Salzburg, Universität, Institut für Slawistik.
SLAWISTISCHE BIBLIOTHEK. Halle, Niemeyer.
SPECIMENA PHILOLOGIAE SLAVICAE. München, Sagner.
SPRAAKLIGA BIDRAG. Lund, Seminariet foer Slaviska spraak.
STOCKHOLM SLAVIC STUDIES. Stockholm, Acta Universitatis Stockholmiensis.
STOCKHOLM STUDIES IN RUSSIAN LITERATURE. Stockholm, Almqvist.
STUDIA HISTORICA ET PHILOLOGICA. SECTIO SLAVICA. Firenze, Licosa Editrice.
STUDIA HISTORICA ET PHILOLOGICA. SECTIO SLAVOROMANICA. Firenze, Licosa Editrice.
STUDIA SLAVICA ET BALTICA. Münster, Aaschendorf.
STUDIEN UND TEXTE. Center for the studies of Slavic languages and literatures. The Hebrew Univ. of Jerusalem. Bremen, K-Presse.
STUDIES IN MODERN RUSSIAN LANGUAGE. Cambridge, University Press.
STUDIES IN RUSSIAN EPIC TRADITION. Leiden, E. Brill.
STUDIES IN SLAVIC AND GENERAL LINGUISTICS. Amsterdam, Rodopi.
STUDIES IN SLAVIC LINVISTICS. Edmonton, Alberta University.
STUDIES IN SLAVIC LITERATURE AND POETICS. Amsterdam, Rodopi.

SÜDOSTEUROPÄISCHE ARBEITEN. München, Oldenburg.
SYMBOLAE SLAVICAE. Frankfurt/Main, Lang.
UCLA SLAVIC STUDIES. Columbus, Ohio, Slavica Publ.
UNIVERSITY OF TEXAS PRESS SLAVIC SERIES. Austin, Univ. of Texas Press.
VERÖFFENTLICHUNGEN DES OSTEUROPA INSTITUTS MÜNCHEN. REIHE: GESCHICHTE. Wiesbaden, Harrassowitz.
VERÖFFENTLICHUNGEN DER ABTEILUNG FÜR SLAVISCHE SPRACHEN UND LITERATUREN DES OSTEUROPA INSTITUTS. Berlin, Freie Universität.
VORTRÄGE UND ABHANDLUNGEN ZUR SLAVISTIC. Giessen, W. Schmitz Verlag.
WAR AND SOCIETY IN EAST CENTRAL EUROPE. Boulder, Social Science monographs. New York, distr. by Columbia University Press.
WIENER ARCHIV FÜR GESCHICHTE DES SLAWENTUMS UND OSTEUROPAS. Wien, Böhlau.
WIENER SLAVISTISCHES JAHRBUCH. Wien, Böhlau.
WIENER SLAWISTISCHER ALMANACH. SONDERBAND. Wien, Institut für Slawistik der Univ. Wien, A. Hanson-Love.
WIRTSCHAFTS- UND SOZIALWISSENSCHAFTLICHE OSTMITTELEUROPA STUDIEN. Marburg/Lahn, Herder Institut.
WIRTSCHAFT UND GESELLSCHAFT IN SÜDOSTEUROPA. München, Oldenburg.
WIRTSCHAFTSWISSENSCHAFTLICHE VERÖFFENTLICHUNGEN. Berlin, Freie Universität, Osteuropa Institut.
WIRTSCHAFTSWISSENSCHAFTLICHE FORGE. Berlin, Freie Universität, Osteuropa Institut.
WISCONSIN SLAVIC PUBLICATIONS. Madison, Univ. of Wisconsin Press.
WISSENSCHAFTLICHE BEITRÄGE ZUR GESCHICHTE UND LANDESKUNDE OSTMITTELEUROPAS. Marburg/Lahn, Herder Institut.
YALE RUSSIAN AND EAST EUROPEAN STUDIES. New Haven, Yale Univ. Press.
YALE RUSSIAN AND EAST EUROPEAN PUBLICATIONS. New Haven, Yale Consilium on International and Area studies.

"RUSSICA" BIBLIOGRAPHY SERIES

Access to Resources in the '80s: Proceedings of the First International Conference of Slavic Librarians and Information Specialists. Ed. by Marianna T. Choldin. 110 p. $7.50.

EDWARD KASINEC. Slavic Books and Bookmen. Papers and Essays. 180 p. $13.50.

WOJCIECH ZALEWSKI. Russian-English Dictionaries with Aids for Translators. A Selected Bibliography. 144 p. $7.50.

WOJCIECH ZALEWSKI. Fundamentals of Russian Reference Work in the Humanities and in Social Sciences. 170 p. $13.50.

EUGENE J. KISLUK and EUGENE BESHENKOVSKY, EDS. Vive la Pologne! The Henryk Gierszynski Collection. Ca. 500 p.

BOSILJKA STEVANOVIC and VLADIMIR WERTSMAN. Free Voices in Russian Literature, 1950s — 1980s: A Bio-Bibliographical Guide. Ca. 500 p.

Wojciech Zalewski
Fundamentals of Russian Reference Work
in the Humanities and Social Sciences
Printed in USA